The Last Wilderness

The Last Wilderness

600 miles by canoe and portage in the Northwest Territories

Peter Browning

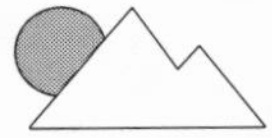

GREAT WEST BOOKS LAFAYETTE, CALIFORNIA

Second Edition. First Edition published 1975

Cover design by Larry Van Dyke and Peter Browning
Front cover photo: Author portaging past cascades on the Eileen River

Printed in the United States of America

Great West Books
PO Box 1028
Lafayette, CA 94549

Library of Congress Cataloging-in-Publication Data

Browning, Peter, 1928–
The last wilderness : 600 miles by canoe and portage in the Northwest Territories / Peter Browning. — 2nd ed.
p. cm.
Bibliography: p.
ISBN 0–944220–03–7 (alk. paper)
1. Great Slave Lake Region (N.W.T.)—Description and travel. 2. Mackenzie (N.W.T.)—Description and travel. 3. Keewatin (N.W.T.)—Description and travel. 4. Canoes and canoeing—Northwest Territories. 5. Browning, Peter, 1928– —Journeys—Northwest Territories. 6. Northwest Territories—Description and travel–Bibliography. I. Title.
F1100.G8B76 1989
917.19′2—dc19 88–82711
CIP

Contents

Illustrations

Preface

The first edition of *The Last Wilderness* was published in 1975 by Chronicle Books, San Francisco. It has been out of print for twelve years.

This second edition has the same text, except for some altered syntax and a few minor changes in wording. The appearance of the two editions is quite different. The first edition was in an 8 x 9 format rather than the 7 x 10 of this edition. The first had two columns of text on a page, whereas the second has one. This edition has an additional eleven photographs, and all of the comments in the left margins are new. I have also added a northern bibliography, which I hope will serve to guide readers to the fascinating literature of exploration, travel, and adventure in the mainland Northwest Territories.

My friend Malcolm E. Barker, himself an author and publisher (Londonborn Publications), generously provided advice and beneficial criticism concerning the design of both the text pages and the cover. He was always available for consultation, and offered many invaluable ideas—ideas that I was not having for myself.

George Luste of the Physics Department at the University of Toronto, and Stuart Mackinnon of the History Department, University of Alberta, helped me with the northern bibliography, correcting my errors and filling in the gaps and omissions.

It is quite likely that I never would have gone to the North—or certainly not done so by canoe—had I not met John Blunt in the spring of 1964, just ten weeks before we embarked on this trip. My profound thanks goes to John, for he showed me the way to the North.

Introduction

When John Blunt and I made this canoe journey twenty-five years ago, in 1964, vacation canoe travel in the Northwest Territories had scarcely begun. Eric Morse and his party had gone from Sifton Lake down the Hanbury and Thelon rivers in 1962. They were, as he wrote, "the first Canadian recreational canoeists to have crossed the full breadth of the Barren Lands."

Now it is a common thing. Significant numbers of people have been on the Thelon, the Dubawnt, the Coppermine, and other once-remote rivers in the North. But in 1964 we felt that we were going off into the great unknown—almost without predecessors, and with a sense of excitement and trepidation. It was our expectation, which was fulfilled, that we would see no other people during the trip.

My one regret was that we found it necessary to kill two game animals—a moose and a caribou—and we also took a number of grouse and fish. What we did was illegal, and we certainly do not advocate that anyone should emulate us. It is neither desirable nor recommended that those who go north should do so with the intention of living off the land.

There is nothing to compare with such a journey as ours. Much of life in the modern world consists of doing things one would rather not do, but under the rules, conditions, and strictures that we have imposed upon ourselves we are obliged to do them. Readers of this book perhaps may feel that we sacrificed too much to achieve our hearts' desire—that the labor, discomfort, and hardship were not worth the candle. But that would be quite wrong. We could not have done better for ourselves. All the signs are positive.

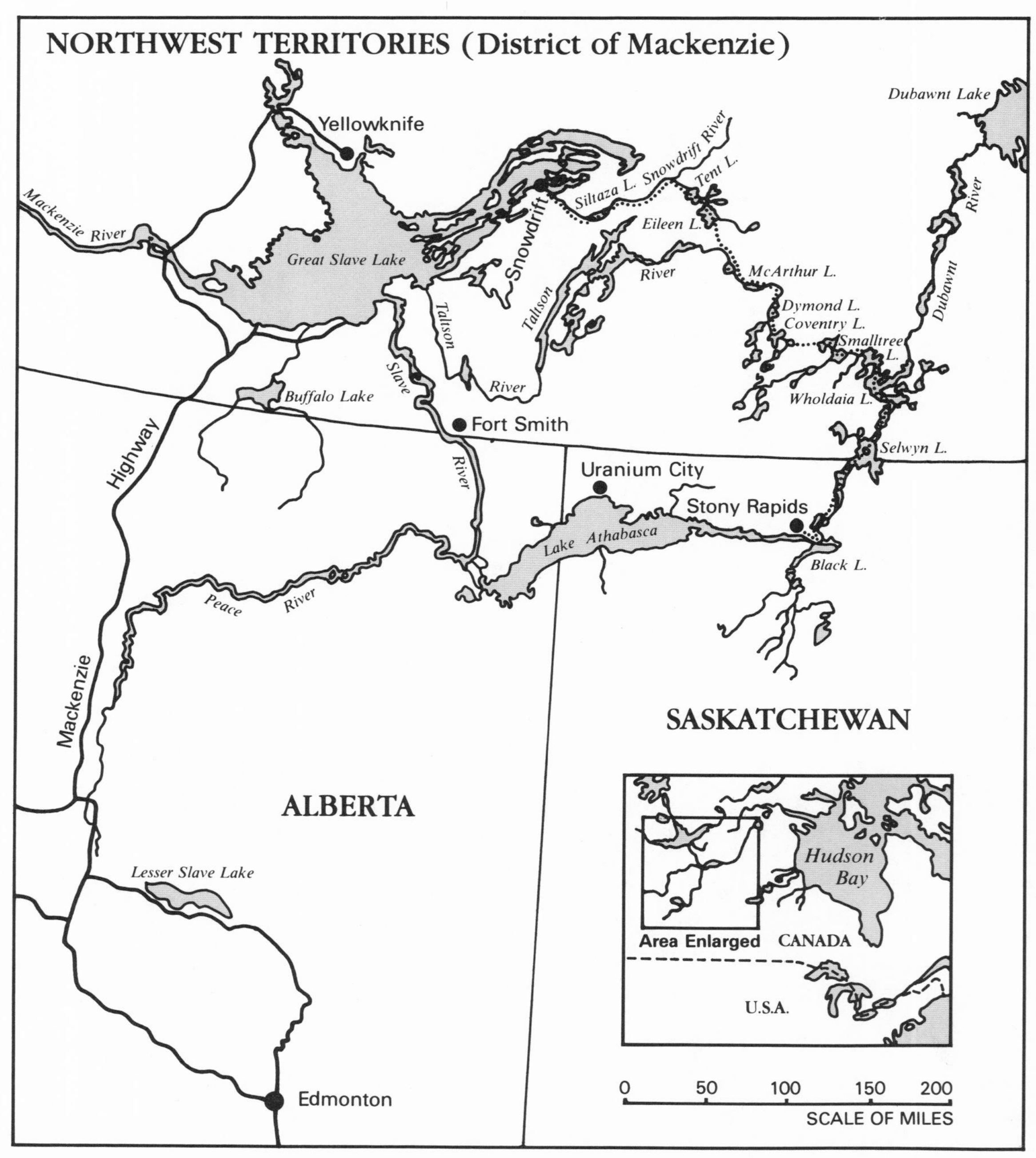
NORTHWEST TERRITORIES (District of Mackenzie)
Yellowknife
Mackenzie River
Great Slave Lake
Snowdrift
Siltaza L.
Snowdrift River
Tent L.
Eileen L.
Dubawnt Lake
Dubawnt River
McArthur L.
Dymond L.
Coventry L.
Smalltree L.
Wholdaia L.
Selwyn L.
Taltson River
Slave River
Buffalo Lake
Fort Smith
Uranium City
Stony Rapids
Lake Athabasca
Black L.
Peace River
Mackenzie Highway
SASKATCHEWAN
ALBERTA
Lesser Slave Lake
Edmonton
Hudson Bay
Area Enlarged
CANADA
U.S.A.
0 50 100 150 200
SCALE OF MILES

A Time to Roam

The last wilderness

NORTH OF THE SIXTIETH PARALLEL, east of Great Slave Lake, and west of Hudson Bay is an immense sweep of pure, unspoiled land. It is the least accessible region in North America, a wilderness that has been seen by few and traversed by fewer still, and is inhabited by no one. There is only the land, carved and molded by the glaciers: scoured boulders, ridges and low hills of white sand, the sparkling waters of myriad lakes.

It was summer. John Blunt and I would travel across this territory by canoe, out of contact with civilization for eleven weeks as we paddled and portaged our way through 600 miles of uninhabited wilderness. We would be alone; should we meet disaster there would be no salvation.

I had met John just ten weeks earlier. I first heard his name, and about his proposed canoe trip, in casual conversation with a friend over a glass of beer. John, a geologist by profession but a wanderer and wilderness man by inclination, had placed notices on the bulletin boards of various universities and colleges in Los Angeles, seeking three or more men to accompany him. He and I exchanged letters, met a week later, and hit it off at once. It quickly became apparent that on such short notice we would not be able to find other compatible men interested in and capable of undertaking so long and strenuous a journey. We began at once to lay plans for just the two of us.

John and I are kindred souls in many ways, and we have a yearning to run off to whatever remote and untamed places still exist. There, although obliged to perform the most arduous labors, we are more in harmony with our surroundings and are leading more coherent lives than we find possible in the technological milieu. Our lives are stifled by the environment of steel, stone, and glass that has sprouted all around us with such fantastic speed. In the wilderness we can revel in pure nature—or, if we so desire, wallow in it.

North to Edmonton

The trip by car from Los Angeles brought us across the California and Nevada deserts, through Idaho, around the southern boundary of Glacier National Park in Montana, and north through Calgary to Edmonton. The car was heavily loaded. We had with us all our personal gear for the trip—John's two rifles, a suitcase apiece containing the clothes for wearing in Edmonton and when we returned at the end of the summer, ninety pounds of dehydrated food, and two large boxes. The boxes, built by ourselves of one-half- and three-quarter-inch plywood, were thirty by sixteen by twenty-two inches, and would be used for carrying canned goods, cooking utensils, fishing tackle, axes, camp shovel, and the rest of our hardware. In Edmonton we purchased three Woods bags—large canvas packsacks—in which to tote the Dri Lite dehydrated food and our clothing. We also bought, at surplus stores in California, about two dozen rubberized, waterproof bags of various sizes into which we placed all clothing, food, and anything else that might be damaged by water. We packed the bags in the boxes and Woods bags, and they plus the canoe constituted the six loads we carried on portages. The canoe, rented from the Hudson's Bay Company, was awaiting us at the company's post at Black Lake in northern Saskatchewan. Unlike the northern travelers of old, we took neither alcohol nor tobacco. A spot of booze might have gone well on a cold evening, but its bulk and weight made it not worth the effort. As for tobacco, John did not smoke except for an occasional cigarette after a meal or with drinks, and I had kicked the habit seven months earlier.

The route

John had made reservations for the flights that would take us from Edmonton to our starting point, and had procured from the Canadian government the necessary maps—plus aerial photographs of those areas where the maps were not sufficiently detailed. John had been in Alaska and northern Canada and had considerable canoeing experience, but I had not been in the North and was a neophyte at canoe travel.

Our route ran north-northeast from Black Lake—first up the Chipman River and a chain of lakes to Wholdaia Lake and the watershed of the Dubawnt River. There the route turned westward, up the Dubawnt to Smalltree Lake, thence west-northwest to the headwaters of the Taltson River, down the Taltson for more than 100 miles, north across a height of land to Eileen Lake and the upper Snowdrift River, and then west-southwest down the Snowdrift to our objective, the Indian village and Hudson's Bay Company trading post of Snowdrift on an eastern arm of Great Slave Lake.

Unknown country

The route from Black Lake to Wholdaia Lake and the Dubawnt River was first traveled by white men in 1893. At that time the Tyrrell brothers, with a party of three Iroquois Indians from Québec and three half-breeds, went on from Wholdaia Lake down the Dubawnt River to Baker Lake and Chesterfield Inlet, on the northwest coast of Hudson Bay. James W. Tyrrell was a botanist, and J. Burr Tyrrell, a geologist. They made a geographical and topographical survey for the Canadian government, examined the geology along their route, and collected specimens of the flora. In his account of the journey, James Tyrrell wrote: "Of almost this entire territory less was known than of the remotest districts of 'Darkest Africa,' and, with but few exceptions, its vast and dreary plains had never been trodden by the foot of man, save that of the dusky savage." Even the "dusky savage" had only the vaguest idea of the nature of the country that lay beyond a few days' journey from Black Lake. The Indians seldom ventured into the Barren Lands for fear they would encounter their mortal enemies the Eskimos. An area of more than 200,000 square miles was so little known that the Tyrrells were not certain whether the Dubawnt River flowed to Hudson Bay or to the Arctic Ocean. After the Tyrrells' expedition the territory remained essentially untraveled for more than half a century. No one went down the Dubawnt River again until 1955, when a party of six Americans led by Arthur Moffatt, an explorer and photographer, traveled the same route from Black Lake to Baker Lake.

Guy Blanchet, a surveyor for the Canadian government, explored the Smalltree Lake area in 1917; he also went down the lower Snowdrift River in 1925. Of the rest of our route we knew nothing other than what our maps could tell us. It had rarely been traveled, and apparently never by anyone who kept a written record of it.

Heavy duty

The weight of our outfit, which went with us as freight on the flight from Edmonton, was 463 pounds. It cost us $14.50 per hundred pounds to get it to Uranium City, and another $7.00 per hundred from there to Stony Rapids, a Hudson's Bay post and landing strip seventeen miles from Black Lake. We were stunned by the weight; it was a hundred pounds more than we had anticipated. My muscles ached at the very thought of hauling all that stuff around.

There was nothing left to do but make the most of our remaining time in town. We ate a hearty dinner, took in a movie, drank a couple of beers, and spent our last night under a roof and in beds for the next eleven weeks. If the actual trip turned out to be as good as the anticipation of it, we would have a superb season.

But summers are short, and for each of us growing fewer in number. It was a time for action. We were primed to go.

Where we were headed. Lakes and tundra, near the treeline.

Departure

June 10

WE LAY IN OUR BEDS as long as possible in the morning, luxuriating in those blissful moments between sleep and full wakefulness—the most peaceful, untroubled time of day. A plane from the nearby airport, roaring over our motel like a guttural, mechanical prophecy of our departure, brought us fully awake at once, our heads whirling with a welter of last-minute details. The contemplation and avid anticipation of the trip—such a delight when we were in California—had been lost in two days of frenzied shopping and packing. The profusion of purchases and trivial but necessary arrangements had combined to temporarily squelch our passion for the journey. We both were nervous and irritable.

We cope with things economic and material because we must, but in essence we are romantics and dreamers. Though our minds were intent on the complexities of our arrangements, our hearts ran away to the tranquil emptiness and simplicity of the North.

Nostalgia for the future

Ever since I met John he had bombarded me with rapturous descriptions of the northern wilderness and glowing prophecies of the aesthetic and emotional satisfaction, the sense of purpose, and a "meaning" to life that he hoped to find on the journey. John had created quite a mystique of the North, and had managed to instill in me nostalgia for a place I had never seen. Yet only three months earlier I had not so much as imagined such a trip. I had a chance meeting, a casual conversation, made a quick decision, and set off in a radical new direction—a departure from everything that had gone before.

The morning was clear, warm, and calm, a perfect day for beginning the greatest adventure of our lives. The moment of departure neared. We were intoxicated by the swiftly approaching release from the cares of the mundane world, drunk on dreams of escape and boundless freedom. All our burdens could be sloughed off like outgrown clothing, and the demoralizing tumult of civilized life soon forgotten. Perhaps we would be able to cut life down to size and make it comprehensible in human terms.

Stealing away

We ate breakfast in a nearby restaurant. Already we felt set apart from the others who were there. While we flew away to a summer of freedom, they would still be enmeshed in the dull normality of everyday life—the humdrum routine of home and job that struck us as so utterly stifling. There was a fleeting impulse to crow about our coming voyage and to commiserate with all those others over their misfortune, but we managed to quell it. It was best to keep the trip a secret; a small part of our pleasure was in stealing away unnoticed.

When we checked in at the airport we had ninety-five pounds of baggage with us. The allowance was forty pounds each, so we had to pay an excess-baggage charge. But money no longer mattered. If our expenses suddenly had doubled we would have spent the money without a qualm. Money had ceased to be the obsession and absolute necessity it is in our civilization; it had become simply a commodity, something to be exchanged for the privilege of going north. John was carrying a spare paddle, not wanting to entrust it to the baggage handlers. Our values were changing; the paddle was something that was fine and precious that needed to be treated with tender loving care. It was a relief to be leaving the car and other complications behind. If we did not rip a hole in the canoe or break a paddle, we would always be assured of transportation.

Changing values

Our flight took off on time, bound for Yellowknife with an intermediate stop at Fort Smith where we would transfer to the plane to Uranium City. Twenty minutes out of Edmonton the countryside below changed from neatly squared-off farms to clearings interspersed with patches of forest. There was an increasing number of lakes, long and narrow ones running north-south, looking as though they had been scratched out of the rock by gigantic fingernails. A plume of gray smoke rose from a brush fire and drifted northward. The last remnants of man's handiwork faded away. To the north and east of us was a vast wilderness, unblemished by buildings or roads, not yet torn or scarred by bulldozers. And perhaps it never will be, for the climate is harsh and the land yields grudgingly and offers little sustenance.

The stewardess passed down the aisle, serving tea and coffee and distributing magazines. I browsed through a copy of *Newsweek*. On the cover was a Picasso painting of the kind that had become a trademark: geometrical figures looking as though they would explode or disintegrate under inhuman stress or tension; faces split down the middle, the halves confronting each other with wide staring eyes that had lost the ability to laugh or weep. The figures and faces seemed possessed of immense power and energy, but would never use it; they were immobile, frozen. It was the husk of the calm, benign, bright schizophrenia of the Western world. And we were leaving it.

Abstract Nature

From the air the terrain looked like an immense abstract painting done in varying shades of gray and green, with occasional clumps of dull wet brown and blobs of faintly electric blue thrown on the canvas at random. Individual ponds caught my attention with their sparkles when the angle of the sun was right.

What we would find in the North we did not know—certainly not wealth or acclaim. We told ourselves that we wished to escape, however briefly, from the demands and pressures of a garish, frenetic, artificial society; that we wanted to cope with nature on her own terms; that we were eager to explore new territory and travel through a wilderness that few men had ever seen. Then too, there was the urge to prove to ourselves that we could undertake a journey of such dimensions and bring it off successfully. But perhaps those were only rationalizations for the expedition, and the true reasons—and their implications—were hidden from us. Above all, we needed the time and space and leisure to contemplate our world and ourselves.

Fort Smith

We had a two-hour wait at Fort Smith for our flight to Uranium City. This was time enough for John to take a taxi into town to the Department of Northern Affairs and Natural Resources. He had a geological hammer and a prospector's license, and wanted to get some of the metal tags required for staking claims.

The taxi drivers were Indians. In the short time of one or two generations the Indians have come from a nomadic life of hunting and trapping to a marginal existence on the fringes of the white man's wage and money economy. Whether they have made a good bargain is a moot point. Their culture has been subverted and left in a shambles by the savage power of the white man's economic system and by the militant proselytizing of the missionaries. Most of what gives a people an identity, a coherent reason for living, a quality and character all their own, has been forgotten or destroyed. The old myths, beliefs, and immemorial tales are already dead or swiftly dying. Those who have survived this process are the inheritors of a moribund culture; theirs is a legacy of blasted hopes and ruined lives. The best they can hope for is that the continuing and irresistible process of social and cultural mutation will be accomplished with a minimum of pain.

Subversion

John returned with the word that tags for the area of our travels must be procured in Yellowknife. So much for that; bureaucracy won again. We wouldn't be in Yellowknife until the trip was over and we were on our way back to Edmonton.

We left for Uranium City on a C–46, having been assured that our outfit was safely stored in the cargo compartment. A DC–3 was waiting for us at Uranium City when we landed there after a one-hour flight. We quickly transferred our gear, and were off again. The flight to the dusty landing strip at Stony Rapids took forty minutes. The moment the engines stopped and the door was opened, John was out and running down the dirt road to the Hudson's Bay Company store. He was brimming with nervous energy, and was anxious to take care of the last details so that we could be away. We talked to Walitski, the manager, and were gratified to learn that he had been thorough and obliging. Our canoe was waiting for us at Black Lake, and there was no longer anything to stop us.

Stony Rapids

John was familiar with the area, having spent the summer of 1962 there as a member of a geological survey crew. While I wandered around the store to see what we should buy, John visited the corporal of the Royal Canadian Mounted Police, traced our route on the corporal's map, and told him that we expected to reach Snowdrift between August 25 and September 1. If we weren't there by September 1 they would come looking for us. That is, they would fly our route.

Thinking the unthinkable

But if we should come to grief at an unknown location on a route of some 600 miles, the chances of being found were slim. Like everyone else, though, we had confidence in our ability to stay alive. We had discussed, seriously and at length, the possibility that we might not return from the journey. The hazards were many; severe injury or illness could prove fatal once we were well advanced on the trip and beyond the hope of quick rescue. As John succinctly put it, it's conceivable that we would be "wiped out." But death while we were engaged in something as valuable to us as this journey, would be far more meaningful than to be killed in a traffic accident or in some equally absurd manner.

Although we forced ourselves to think about the extinction of our lives and the possibility that it might come that summer, we couldn't believe it would happen. We're like almost everyone else in this respect. Intellectually we know we will die some day, but secretly we are certain we will live forever. Giving our route to the corporal was mainly a matter of complying with regulations, and only secondarily a means of hedging our bet.

Fond du Lac River

The store faced the Fond du Lac River, which flows westward into Lake Athabasca. Before the days of air travel, that was the route followed by anyone wishing to go north in this region. The Tyrrell brothers came that way from Edmonton in 1893, a journey requiring five weeks—which we covered in half a day. Moffatt and his crew gathered there in 1955, then were driven by truck to Black Lake and set out from there, as we would do.

I bought fifty feet of clothesline, and four loaves of bread to go with the two we already had. The store was the focal point of activity. Eight or ten Indians were standing around inside. Most of them did not seem to be buying anything; the store served mainly as a place to meet and gossip. Several young men were sitting on a railing out front, like the town loafers on a courthouse bench. Did they sit there because they were at peace with the world and because sitting was one of the pleasures of life? Or was it that their lives were so empty and meaningless that no interest could arouse them? Unfortunately we couldn't stay long enough to find out. There they sat, observing the local happenings, and pondering—what? Us, perhaps—two incomprehensible white men coming north with a mountain of gear, and in a great hurry. But why hurry? Ah, we can't help it. Hurry is indelibly engraved on our nervous systems.

Going to Black Lake

We thanked Walitski for his assistance, then climbed into the cab of the old International truck and hurried off toward Black Lake. There was no road connection to the outside world. The half dozen vehicles there had been flown in, and all traffic was strictly local. The road had not yet been worked on that season and was quite rough in places; nevertheless we pounded over the bumps and slithered through stretches of

Shades of Art Moffatt

sand at a good clip. The truckdriver was a half-breed, the son of the owner of the truck. John asked him if he had ever heard of Moffatt. He turned out to be the driver, with the same truck, who carried Moffatt to Black Lake in 1955. He had a disconcerting habit of talking about Moffatt and his crew in the present tense, as though he had driven them over the road that morning and they had yet to make their trip.

"That guy," he said, "he don't know what he's doing. He's got too much gear. You know, he's got a lot of hardtack. Everybody says you should take flour and not hardtack."

"He didn't make it," said John. "He fell in the water and froze to death up in the Barrens."

"That wouldn't surprise me any," said the driver. "He's starting too late. It's too long a trip."

I couldn't tell if he knew of Moffatt's death and was having it reconfirmed, or if he was hearing about it for the first time. Or perhaps he was foretelling the future.

"Well," said John, "he's dead now. But the rest of them got there okay."

"He's got a big box full of picture-taking stuff," said the driver. "And all that hardtack. You got any hardtack?"

"Just flour," said John. "We make bannock."

"That bannock is pretty good when you're hungry," said the driver. "But you'd never catch me with any hardtack. It's too heavy. I don't think you'll get there if you take all that. How come somebody wants to go that far?"

"I don't know," said John. "We just like to do it."

We bounced along in silence after that. There wasn't anything else to say.

When we pulled up in front of the Black Lake Hudson's Bay post at six, there were a few boys playing down by the dock, and no one else in sight. We introduced ourselves to the manager, a Scotsman named Mackenzie, and inspected our aluminum canoe, which was stored in the warehouse. The "fancy tin canoe," Mackenzie called it. He was an outspoken, jovial fellow,

The grave of Art Moffatt, at Baker Lake, Northwest Territories.

talking with a rich burr and carrying a heavy, gnarled walking stick. The Hudson's Bay Company still does considerable recruiting in Scotland—partly, it seems, to find people temperamentally suited to a life of isolation and few entertainments.

"The fancy tin canoe." John and our pile of gear, on the beach at Black Lake.

Getting the onceover

The canoe was a seventeen-foot Grumman, equipped with a carrying yoke, three ash paddles, and an aluminum repair kit. It had a beam of thirty-six inches, a center depth of thirteen and a third inches, and weighed seventy-five pounds. We quickly became the focus of attention, or rather the truck with our outfit in it did. One by one the men of the settlement showed up and gathered in a semicircle at the back of the truck to scrutinize our gear and, apparently, to pass judgment among themselves as to its quality and practicality. Our arrival at the post, and imminent departure, was a major event. Undoubtedly we would be a topic of conversation long after we were gone. Yet even though the Indians were intensely curious, none of them rushed to examine our gear. They sauntered slowly in the general direction of the truck, hands stuffed in pockets, seeming to be monumentally detached and to be arriving at the truck only by accident. No one hurried. Either they wished to appear unimpressed and sufficiently sophisticated to take that sort of thing in their stride, or, more likely, they couldn't conceive of any reason for haste.

Time is circular

Life in such an environment is essentially timeless. The sense of long spans of time scarcely exists; what happened ten years ago may be spoken of as though it were only yesterday. Time is circular rather than linear. There are night and day, the changing seasons, and a lifetime divided into childhood, prime, and old age, rather than being counted year by year as is done in societies driven by clock and calendar. Everything is born, lives, dies, and is born anew: an eternal sequence of growth, decline, and resurrection.

In the machine world whence we had come, time has risen on a long inclined plane from the primordial past to the present moment, and is fated to continue onward and upward to some distant, imaginary goal. Time rushes past and can never be recaptured. But in the North there are no time clocks to punch, no anxiety at the thought of time fleeting by and lost forever. There is no weight of years: the only reality is now.

The Northern Stores Department of the Hudson's Bay Company is still essentially a feudal institution in relation to its employees and the Indians. Mackenzie ruled over his domain with a benevolent but firm hand. He had two assistants, young men up for the summer to serve as apprentice clerks. Mackenzie invited John and me and the truckdriver to dinner. The apprentices prepared and served the meal, while the rest of us took our ease and ate our fill.

When Mackenzie learned that we were from California he wanted to know about Los Angeles in general and the freeway system in particular. I described the horrendous developments of the automobile age, leaving the impression that all of Los Angeles was paved with concrete, and that every inch of space was desperately fought for by an infinite number of vehicles. Then we hashed over matters of local

Bragging on the North

interest: how cold it was last winter, and weather in general; when the ice went out on the lake—the consensus was that it was May 28, unusually early since the winter was relatively mild; that the mosquitoes weren't as bad that year as in other years; that the black flies were the worst of the insects, but only when present in large numbers. There were fish stories of doubtful veracity, and speculation and theorizing about the presence or absence of moose and caribou for the past several seasons. All of these things were avidly discussed with much boisterous humor. These are the eternal concerns of the North: weather, insects, game, and fish. A great deal of pride was derived from having endured colder weather or suffered the depredations of more vicious swarms of insects than others had, or from being able to tell a good story about someone else who had suffered or endured.

Dismay

Much to our dismay the two boxes did not quite fit into the canoe as planned. The canoe was divided into four compartments by thwarts. We had to put a box into each of the center compartments rather than both in the rearward one, and jam the Woods bags in as best we could. One of the bags wound up in the rear compartment, directly in front of John. Several hours at a stretch with the bag sitting practically in his lap would likely give him a feeling akin to claustrophobia. But it couldn't be helped. Not only were the boxes an inch too wide, but the bags were so bulky that we couldn't get more than two in a compartment. Then there were two rifles, two spare paddles, two pack frames, and John's huge sleeping bag—which we fitted in only with great difficulty.

A critical audience

The Hudson's Bay men, the truckdriver, and the Indian men and boys stood on the dock and observed our loading procedure. The truckdriver shook his head in disapproval. "You got too much gear," he said. "You gotta throw one of those boxes away." That was out of the question; nor were we in the mood to accept unsolicited advice. We wanted to load and leave as quickly as possible. Not only did we wish to make a few miles, but we were disconcerted by the critical gaze of our audience. We were fearful of committing some dreadful *faux pas* that would disgrace us in the eyes of the community.

Disgrace

The only disgrace fell on a hapless Indian boy who was accidentally jostled off the dock into shallow water. He was soaked but unharmed. Some of the men helped him back onto the dock where he stood silently for a moment as if too stunned to react, then burst into helpless and outraged tears. The other Indians indulged in a big laugh at his expense; it was their only display of emotion while we were there. They are a phlegmatic people, at least in the presence of strangers. No one attempted to comfort the boy; the louder he sobbed the more they all laughed. The boy undoubtedly was certain the mishap had spoiled his entire summer—if not, indeed, his life.

John and I managed a partly satisfactory loading, but the canoe was low in the water, top-heavy, and felt a bit unstable.

We estimated that we and our gear together weighed somewhat more than 900 pounds. Too much! We had to resist the impulse to throw away what might have appeared to be excess food or superfluous equipment. But from everything we had ever heard or read, that seems to have been the experience of every expedition or extended journey: either they were badly underequipped or grossly overburdened. We admonished each other to eat heartily for a few weeks to cut down the weight.

Overloaded

We paid the truckdriver twelve dollars for the ride from Stony Rapids, our last financial dealing for the next eleven weeks—too bad it wasn't the last financial transaction of our lives. Then we stashed away our remaining cash and traveler's checks, and forgot about the fool stuff.

On our way

We shoved off a few more minutes before eight. The sky was overcast and the water calm. The only sounds were the splash of our paddles and the gurgle of water beneath our canoe. Although it was a gray, somber evening, I was exultant and giddy—rather like the way one feels when a roller coaster swoops down that first steep hill.

My canoeing experience consisted of several brief turns on a small lake in New Hampshire when I was a boy. I was quite unsure of myself, and I was relying on John to have the necessary know-how to see us through. In 1954 he went alone down the Albany River in Ontario from Sioux Lookout to the mouth of the river at Fort Albany on James Bay, a distance of about 500 miles. With that much experience under his belt he would certainly know what he was about.

But at the moment experience was not our major concern. Sedentary life hadn't prepared me for such labor. I was not able to paddle steadily for more than ten or fifteen minutes at a stretch, by which time my arms felt like dead weights. After a thirty-second break I would dig in again, but paddling was going to be rough work until I put on some muscle.

By 10:30 we had made eight and a half miles, and we camped on the south side of a sandy point. In spite of the overcast we were able to see perfectly well when we turned in at midnight.

It had been a long day, one that we had anticipated so much it might have been anticlimactic. But the change, in only twelve hours, from Edmonton to the shores of Black Lake, had been so abrupt and complete that it couldn't help but penetrate even a dulled consciousness and rouse the sense of exhilaration again.

More Alive Than Ever

June 11

IT WAS STRANGE to awaken in a low, narrow tent. It took me a moment before I figured out where I was. Immediately I was anxious to be up and away. But since we had no established routine, and our gear was packed for weight distribution and compactness rather than convenience, it was quite some time before we located what we needed for breakfast. We had a meal of fruit, oatmeal, and tea.

Our tent was a two-man, army-surplus, nylon affair, World War II vintage. It was five feet wide and six feet, eight inches long, just barely large enough to accommodate both of us. Something larger would have provided greater comfort, but having a small, lightweight tent was more important than luxury. It was supposedly waterproof, but we didn't want to rely too heavily on a piece of material that had been in storage for a quarter century. As added protection we had a nine-by-ten-foot canvas fly. After erecting the tent we cut a slender tree for a ridgepole, then draped the fly over the pole and anchored it firmly to the ground and the ends of the pole. The fly completely covered the tent, and provided about a foot and a half of overhang all the way around.

The low ridge on the west side of the lake bore patches of light and dark green foliage—the lighter, birch, and the darker, black spruce, by far the predominant tree in that region. A mature forest is composed almost entirely of spruce, and the patches of spruce and birch alternate because the areas have been burned at different times. Fireweed and other shrubs are the first new growth in a burned-over forest, followed several years later by birch. In a few decades the slower-starting spruce takes over, and the birch is relegated to the shores of lakes and other open places where it can get more sun. Eventually trees die and fall to the ground, dry wood and brush accumulate, a fire cleans it out again—and the forest starts anew. The complete cycle may take several hundred years: an eternal sequence of growth, decline, and resurrection.

Follow the ice

The first day's fine start had us in good spirits, although it was too bad we couldn't have come up a week or ten days earlier. One of John's maxims about travel in the North is "follow the ice." Ideally, one should be poised to leave at a moment's notice, and should start out on the very day the ice breaks up. Summer in the North is too short for any of it to be frittered away. In 1955 Moffatt, because of a delay in his supply arrangements, did not leave the Black Lake post until July 2. We had a twenty-two-day start on that schedule, and were in good shape as far as time was concerned.

John spent several hours punching four small holes in the gunwales on each side of the canoe. He installed wire loops in the holes and tied rope to the loops so that we could crisscross the loaded canoe to be sure that everything stayed

Loaded and ready to go. Black Lake, the second morning. Fir Island in the distance.

in should we capsize. I puttered around with the boxes and bags, shuffling various items to make them more accessible and to make the load less top-heavy. But our major concern was the simple fact that the weight was too great. We offered each other platitudes: "Well, it's better to have too much than too little." We both concurred, and we had solved nothing. The only solution to the weight problem was that we would have to use that much more strength to haul our outfit over the portages.

Good thinking

By the time John finished with the hole-punching, the wind had picked up and the lake was quite rough; there were whitecaps on the open water past the point. It was too rough for us. We passed the afternoon looking at maps and talking over details of food, equipment, packing, and loading of the canoe.

The place had been much camped in; there were many cans and other debris lying about. It was an annoyance, but we couldn't expect to find any previously unused campsites on that part of the route. Indians, and more recently white trappers, had inhabited and traveled the region for hundreds of years. There were several tripod pole arrangements over which the Indians drape canvas. There was also a trapper's "tilt," a small flatroofed shelter built of logs with a sandbank as the back wall. It was old and appeared unused; the heyday of the white trappers is past.

Overcoming reality

Another one of John's maxims has it that "the wind dies down at sundown." Generally true, so we hoped that we could get away in the evening and make it up to the beginning of the Chipman portage. The whitecaps seemed as numerous as ever, but after the maxim had been repeated a few times it became strong enough to overcome reality. We wanted it to be calmer; therefore it was. About 7:30 we started out, perversely acting against our own better judgment. No sooner did we round the point and head northeast than we found ourselves bucking heavy swells and a stiff wind. After nearly an hour's paddling, during which we made little better than a mile and shipped a bit of water over the bow, it was plain to see that the wind was not dying down and that we were running considerable risk. Also it was damned uncomfortable. The water was frigid; it felt as though the ice had melted only a few hours before. Flying spray soaked my pants from the knees down, and my hands were frozen into claws. There was no advantage gained from plowing along in a miserable and precarious state, so we headed into shore and made camp.

We were not tired, but we felt frustrated. It was annoying to be prepared for great doings and then have to settle for such a modest advance. Our morale was high, though. We were where we wanted to be, living the sort of life that appealed to us. The last sight of the evening was a flight of ducks going north between the mainland and Fir Island—a silent wavering line of black shadows faintly visible against a dark green forest.

June 12

I SLEPT POORLY last night. I had cold feet and cold knees. My sleeping bag, an old and well-worn mummy type, was not heavy enough for any temperature under fifty degrees. I had had my doubts about the bag, but buried them under a load of unfounded optimism, convincing myself that it would serve me well. It was what I had, and I didn't want to invest in a new one. I should have known better, having already spent many a cold, distressing night while backpacking in the mountains. I had to sleep wearing clothing to compensate for my inadequate bag. It was my own fault, and I cursed myself roundly.

The millionaires

There were many powerboats going up the lake in the morning, carrying the "sportsmen" and their Indian boat operators and guides from one of the two nearby fishing camps. John contemptuously referred to them as "the millionaires," and characterized them as being "widget manufacturers from Peoria." Eight or ten of them were on the plane with us from Uranium City to Stony Rapids. All were Americans, exuding a loud, carefree camaraderie. They brought with them all the appurtenances of urban living they could carry, including several cases of beer and a case of whiskey. The Hudson's Bay men at the Black Lake post called them "tourists," although they probably thought they were "roughing it"—at seventy-five dollars a day! Fortunately we would leave them behind when we started over the portage.

The most valuable piece of material wealth an Indian can have, as well as an important mark of status and prestige, is an outboard engine—or "kicker" as they are called in the North. John said he had never seen an Indian man paddling a canoe; they consider it both demeaning and rather stupid to work so hard. Only the women paddle now, and this in a people who as recently as thirty or forty years ago were among the world's greatest canoemen.

We had no chance to go in the morning; the wind blew steadily and there were many whitecaps. We had been out less than forty-eight hours, yet already I was becoming accustomed to the new environment. When going into the wilderness my first emotion—as it always had been in the past—was fear. The wilderness was so vast, so lonely, so impersonal. All the physical security and psychological supports of our customary existence were missing. We were forced to rely on our own paltry resources, and to realize again how weak and unprepared we are for struggling against nature with only our bare hands.

A triumph of sorts

In the cities, one has the feeling that man has conquered nature, that the acres of concrete and metal and glass are a triumph of sorts. It is a triumph for organization and collective effort, perhaps, but the individual is no better armed nor more capable of providing for himself. On the contrary, he becomes even less able as time goes by. Witness the Indians, only recently as much a part of the natural environment as men can be, but now losing their old skills and becoming dependent on kickers, gasoline, and cash wages to buy superfluous goods that quickly become necessities.

My fear soon passed. If we were careful the waters would not open to swallow us, nor would some dreadful force fall on us out of the sky. We didn't want to conquer nature, merely to exist in it for a while. The lake glistened in the bright sun, the wind rushed through the forests of slender, straight spruce and birch, and we were as free as we would ever be.

The life of a dog

The wind lessened by midafternoon. We broke camp and started out at once. As we got out onto the lake we could hear the mournful howling of a dog; it sounded as though it came from Fir Island. Dogs are a burden to Indians during the summer, so in the spring their masters will sometimes put them on an island to shift for themselves. If they survive the summer on their own they will be picked up in the fall; if they don't survive—well, there are always other dogs. This may seem cruel, but to the Indians it is the only attitude that makes sense. Their dogs are slaves, and are valued solely for their utility. The only reason for their continued existence is that they pull the Indians' sleds in winter. The dogs spend a lifetime at hard work, and for their pains they are rewarded with the possibility of abandonment when there is no work to do to earn their keep. To the Indians the master-slave relationship must appear right and just. They too are slaves—to the availability of game and fish, the harsh climate, the cash they are paid for however many furs they can trap. To treat dogs as white men treat machines is the natural and logical order of things. In the eyes of an Indian, the "civilized" custom of keeping dogs as pets, feeding them with fancy foods, lavishing affection on them and treating them like lovable children, is abnormal behavior—maudlin, vulgar, and wildly misplaced sentiment.

The Chipman portage was the first and longest of the eight or ten well-established and frequently used portage trails on that part of our route. We had been told that there were several Indian families camped at the mouth of the Chipman River, doing some fishing before going down to the post for the summer.

Easy living

Our arrival at the Indian encampment caused a great uproar among the dogs, but the Indians simply sat tight and watched us. Several small children were playing about the camp, a woman was cooking, another woman was hanging up strips of fish to dry in the sun, and the men were lounging in a tent. On the floor of the tent was an incredible litter of food scraps, articles of clothing, paper, nondescript equipment, and general trash. It looked like an explosion in the city dump. Fortunately the Indians showed no inclination to extend hospitality, so we were not obliged to enter the tent.

One of the men spoke and understood a few words of English. He kicked a loose dog out of the way, showed us where the trail began, and led John about 200 yards up the trail to a good landing place for the canoe—a good landing but a bad place to camp. The ground was mushy and there were too many mosquitoes around to suit us. We both had lived for more than a year in almost entirely insect-free southern California, and we felt that *any* mosquitoes were too many. So we carried everything up the trail about a tenth of a mile to some higher ground, leaving behind several pots for hauling water to our dry camp.

The same Indian returned and silently regarded our exertions. He was a short, stocky man—friendly and with a foolish grin plastered on his round face. John and I too were grinning foolishly. It was one of those moments of social embarrassment. No one knew what to say, but eventually we held an inane conversation, like something out of a badly written adventure story for boys.

A dramatic meeting!

Scene: Indian village in the Far North. Red Man meets White.

Red: *Mumble mumble.*

White: *Huh?*

Red: *Mumble mumble.*

White: *What's that?*

Red: (enunciating carefully) *Long portage.*

White: *Yeah, plenty long.*

Red: *How long?*

White: *Three miles.*

Red: *Three miles!*

Topic exhausted. Awkward silence. Red and White grin foolishly. Look intently at nothing. Scuffle feet.

White: *What lake you go to in winter?*

Red: *Silver Lake.*

White: *Silver Lake?*

Red: *Uhm. Silver Lake.*

Topic exhausted. Brief awkward silence. White heaves last heavy load onto back and starts up trail, leaving behind several pots for carrying water to waterless camp.

White: *Well, thanks a lot.* (White walks twenty feet.)

Red: (pointing to pots) *Hey!*

White: (voice loaded with meaning) *I'm coming back.*

White returns shortly. Pots still there. Red man has vanished into mysterious forest.

The dramatic meeting of two cultures! It must be considered a success, though, for we didn't kill each other.

There was a long hard day coming up on the Chipman portage, a chore we had been dreading. This first portage of the trip would be a trial. Our loads would never be heavier nor our muscles flabbier. We were soft and out of condition as the result of much good food and drink and generally easy living.

John at the end of a portage. The canoe with paddles tied inside was the lightest load, but the most awkward.

Away From the Outside

June 13

JOHN HAD PREDICTED good weather for the next day, but it turned out cloudy with occasional sprinkles. No matter; we were anxious to get on with the trip, and were determined to do the portage in anything short of a downpour. The first three days had seemed like a period of preparation and shakedown. Only now were we about to come to grips with the real McCoy. We were brimming with energy and high resolve—or perhaps it was only bravado. In any case, we were going to attack the Chipman portage with all the vigor we could muster.

The burdens of the North

After some more repacking we had our gear organized into six roughly equal loads: three bags, two boxes, and the canoe with four paddles tied inside it. Taking three carries apiece over a three-mile portage meant that we would have to walk fifteen miles: three times across with the loads, and two trips back unloaded. The loads averaged out to approximately 115 pounds each. We had heard tales of Indians who, when need be, portaged with far greater weight—as much as 300 pounds, or even greater loads for very short carries. As far as I was concerned, though, what we had was quite enough.

John bolted the carrying yoke to the canoe, placed it on his shoulders, headed up the trail, and was quickly out of sight. I took one of the Woods bags for my first carry. The bags came equipped with shoulder straps and a "tumpline." The tumpline is a leather strap, fastened to the bag at both ends, which fits across one's forehead. In this way, the neck, when the muscles are properly developed, should take at least half the weight. In the old style of portaging, loads were carried with a tumpline alone—a much more rugged way of doing it, I'm sure. But if the cry should go up, "Where are the men of yesterday?" I would reply that they are most likely dead and buried, made old and killed off prematurely by their extreme exertions.

There is a technique to misery

Before this I had never carried more than fifty-five pounds for any great distance, although that was up and down hill at high altitude. John had tried to prepare me psychologically for the wearisome, laborious toil that is portaging, but he wasn't able to impress upon me what it was actually like. After the first quarter-mile I felt as if my head would be snapped off my shoulders. Or else I would be pulled over backward to lie in a vulnerable and ignominious position, arms and legs waving in the air like those of an inverted beetle, until John returned and helped me up. My impulse was to put down the load and take a long break, but my pride would not let me halt until I got to wherever John had gone with the canoe. Part of the technique of carrying a load with a tumpline is to grasp the line with both hands, near the temples, and maintain a steady pull to take some of the strain off the neck. When I put down a load after a half hour of carrying it, my arms felt as though they would remain permanently bent.

So as not to leave part of our belongings unguarded for long against the Indians' dogs, we took each load roughly halfway across the portage and then returned for the next one. The boxes seemed even heavier and more uncomfortable to carry than the bags. John carried one box with an old army packboard to which he fastened a tumpline. I carried the other one strapped to an aluminum packframe, which was made for toting a narrow-profile pack in the mountains and has a waistband rather than a tumpline to supplement the shoulder straps. It was not meant to carry so heavy and bulky a load. I had to lean forward more than I liked, and when I tightened up on the waistband it felt as though my legs were going to be jammed into the earth. There were a few marshy spots and a bit of uneven footing, but most of the trail was excellent. Moffatt and his party took a day and a half to cover this portage in 1955; we were determined to

do it one day. When the Indians go out in winter they travel by dogsled, a much quicker and easier way to traverse this terrain. Also, as a general rule, the more people in a party the less is the average weight of baggage per person.

Perhaps what we most lacked were a couple of healthy, hefty squaws. Samuel Hearne, in the journal of his travels to the Coppermine River and the Arctic Ocean in 1771 and 1772, quoted his Indian companion and guide, Matonabbee, as saying: "Women were made for labour; one of them can carry, or haul, as much as two men can do. They also pitch our tents, make and mend our clothing, keep us warm at night; and, in fact, there is no such thing as travelling any considerable distance, or for any length of time, in this country, without their assistance. Women, though they do everything, are maintained at a trifling expence; for as they always stand cook, the very licking of their fingers in scarce times is sufficient for their subsistence."

The good old days

Oh, for the good old days! We had neither dogs nor strong women, having elected, even though sound of mind, to do it ourselves—and I could feel the strain. Judging from the way my bones were creaking and my tendons popping, surely we were transporting every ounce of our worldly goods.

We misjudged the distance; the afternoon stretch turned to be longer than the morning one. About half of it was through muskeg—shallow water and muck, studded with two-foot-high hummocks of grass-covered earth. We wore "waders," boots that came halfway to our knees with rubber the first three inches and leather the rest of the way. My feet stayed dry, but the new and very stiff waders rubbed them raw in half a dozen places. The weather improved. There was no rain, and occasionally the sun broke through. But some of the footing was very bad. When I made a misstep or if my feet sank farther into the mud than I expected, I had to lunge forward several steps to keep from falling. And then I stood hunched over, gasping for breath, my legs trembling and the sweat running into my eyes. During the breaks, when my mind might focus on something other than placing one foot in front of the other, I found it incredible that we should treat ourselves in such a harsh fashion. It was one thing to sit in a comfortable chair, sip on a tall cool drink, and contemplate the joys of crashing through the bush and overcoming every obstacle by strength and willpower, and to picture oneself as the all-conquering hero. But the real thing was quite a

The grim today

different story—no heroism, no romance, scarcely anything that could be considered of value. It was just plain hard work. What we needed most of all was an audience—someone to applaud our determination, be awed by our feats, and commiserate with us in our moments of distress. Lacking an appreciative audience, we felt barely capable of performing at all.

By the last leg of the third carry my feet felt like raw hamburger. Perseverance and brute effort finally carried the day. We started at ten in the morning and finished at eight in the evening, both of us by then thoroughly worn. But a good meal set us up again. We were greatly relieved that the Chipman portage was behind us, and we had also gained confidence that we would be able to take our outfit anywhere we wished to go.

After the meal John broke out his fishing gear for the first time. I relaxed and watched the sunset and the trees and the calm lake, listened to the restless, persistent chirping of the birds, and stared into the fire. Fire was not only comfort and convenience and necessity, it was the means by which we felt that we were masters of the situation. We were controlling the environment, bending it to our will and making it perform for us. In civilization, with all the light and heat one desires available at the snap of a switch, there is no such strength and security to be had from so minor a thing as fire. Technological and scientific progress seem capable of supplying endless amounts of power to individuals and societies alike, and at the same time increasing their longing for more power still, always more. But that night I got a far greater sense of power and well-being than ever before from fire. What John and I needed was the symbol and not the actuality of power, and for this the small comfort of a modest fire served quite well. Surely primitive peoples have always felt about fire as I did then. An illusory and deceptive feeling, perhaps, yet it sufficed. All the seeming substance of those wavering, evanescent flames was in a man's mind, but for the moment it served to hold back the immense, unknown, threatening darkness.

Power and security

June 14

WE WERE FULL of aches and pains, and did not arise until 8:30. There was some sun, but a cold wind. Although we were not particularly anxious for another hard day, we planned to do our loafing later on and had to keep going. We were very slow getting away. Our overworked muscles protested and balked, but we forced them to the various tasks and finally shoved the canoe into the water at 11:00. We had only six inches of freeboard at best, and would not be able to venture out into waves of any size. However, waves wouldn't be a concern until we got to the big lakes. There would be much "canoeing" on dry land in the interim.

We were on a small pond for half a mile, then had a portage of forty-five chains. (A chain is a surveyors' measure: sixty-six feet, or eighty chains to the mile.) Forty-five chains was child's play compared with the previous day, but we found that we were lacking in strength and tended to tire quickly.

The calendar said June 14, but spring had just arrived. A patch of snow at the start of the 45-chain portage.

We loaded up again and paddled two miles across Square Lake. The map indicated a small rapids connecting two segments of the lake, but it was drowned out. Next came a portage of three chains. How annoying and tiring it was to have to unload, carry everything 200 feet, then reload. After that we paddled a mile and a half across a lake and made camp at the beginning of the next portage.

The cool weather made our work easier and helped keep the insects down. There were many mosquitoes in marshy areas and around the shores of lakes, but few elsewhere. Among our most important supplies were fifteen bottles of insect repellent. It had seemed to me that we were acquiring a lifetime supply, but John thought it would be barely sufficient to rebuff the hordes of crawling, leaping, flying varmints we expected to encounter later on.

Sunset was about ten o'clock. There was a soft, diffused light hanging gently in the sky and bathing us in a cool red glow. It was always light enough at any time of night to see, or even to read when the sky was clear. One more week until the summer solstice, so we expected to enjoy four or five more weeks of long daylight hours. There were many birds chirping, as if there were no midnight and no tomorrow.

Good clean fun

I became a bit more tired on each successive portage, and recuperated more slowly. We were putting out as much effort in a day as the average workingman expends in a week. But of course this was a vacation; it was good clean fun. Although we had aching muscles and blistered feet, and were fatigued in general, we nevertheless felt blissfully calm and at peace and, above all, felt a pleasant sense of isolation. In just five days we had so radically changed our physical environment and so drastically altered our activities, interests, and entire mode of life that there was no logical connection between what we were doing then and what went before. Our existence in the bush was real—immediate, tangible, completely engrossing. Our former lives, with their strange, inanimate surroundings, seemed composed of nightmare and fantasy.

The joke is on the Outside

Already we referred to that place whence we had come as "the Outside." It was we who were on the inside—in contact with and inside of reality. When we called up memories of mechanized, urban life, we invariably found ourselves making scurrilous jokes and then laughing uproariously at our own wit. It seemed to be the only conceivable way to react to an image of existence that, when viewed from the wilderness, was so strange and grotesque as to make us

wonder what diseased imagination had produced it. And this after only five days! By the time we got to the Outside again we would be even more bemused than Rip Van Winkle.

We congratulated each other on having "escaped," even if it was only for a summer. We had slipped away unnoticed and were now in a part of the world that has remained essentially unchanged since the last ice age—a primordial land thus far spared the inundation of mechanical progress. But we are afraid it can't last. The airplane potentially has opened up everything, and with ever larger numbers of people becoming increasingly affluent, those lakes may someday come to resemble Lake Tahoe or Lake of the Woods or any one of a hundred other places: summer cottages lining the shore, noisy powerboats fouling the air with their exhaust fumes and destroying the shoreline with the waves they kick up, and the inevitable trashy commercialization. If there's money to be made, the entrepreneurs and speculators will come popping out of the woods.

Future ruin

Most men are incapable of reaching a wilderness, no matter how hard they may try. They thrust before them the destructive shockwave of civilization, so that any place at which they arrive—however remote and untrammeled—is spoiled by their presence, spoiled at the very instant of their arrival. John and I took pride in leaving behind us little trace of our passage. All that remained to show that we had come that way were a few ashes at our campsites and the wake of our canoe—which closed in behind us.

June 15

IT WAS a grueling day. First we had a twenty-one-chain portage, then three-fourths of a mile of paddling across a pond, another portage of a third of a mile, half a mile on another pond, and finally a twenty-three-chain portage, which brought us to Chipman Lake. We were ready to fall flat on our faces by the time we finished the last portage, but the camping was no good so we loaded up again and paddled about two miles to a decent site on a sparsely wooded point.

From twenty feet off shore we could hear a high-pitched whine: the warm weather had brought out the mosquitoes in strength. There they were in incredible swarms, doing that mad swirling dance. But repellent kept them away, for the most part, until the cold night air dispersed them. It was my first head-to-head contact with the vaunted mosquito hordes of the North, and I judged their whine to be worse than their bite. There was much frenzied flying about but very little blood-letting. Although I heaped scorn on the mosquitoes for their lack of organization and élan, John insisted that they would soon demonstrate their abilities. Summer is so short in the North that insects run through their entire life cycle in three months or less, and are quiescent for the rest of the year. Such a regimen is enough to make any living thing determined and desperate, but thus far the mosquitoes had shown us only furious confusion. They'll never conquer the world that way.

Weak mosquitoes

John again tried his hand at fishing. Within five minutes he pulled out a twenty-inch trout; just the thing for breakfast on the morrow. He then caught two more, which we admired for a moment and threw back into the lake, feeling magnanimous and virtuous.

At first it seemed as though we spent the day on a treadmill. All I could remember were innumerable trips with the same loads over the same piece of trail. But I felt like a new man once we had relaxed, conversed, and had a bowl of hot soup—the simple pleasures of the poor.

June 16

I WAS BEDRAGGLED both physically and in spirit. After several nights of inadequate sleep everything appeared gloomy. But the trout breakfast improved my outlook, and the prospect of no portaging improved it even more. We took a very long time pulling ourselves together. Many minutes were consumed in wandering about camp in slow motion.

It was my custom to grumble a great deal and curse loudly at aching muscles and heavy work, while John seldom complained about anything. I was not sure whether the aches and heavy labor didn't bother him or whether he considered a stoic silence the best way to overcome such difficulties. Or perhaps he was not aware of the cathartic value of loud griping. I, for one, felt immensely better when I was grousing and moaning about the hardships that beset me.

In an afternoon of steady paddling we covered about sixteen miles to a three-chain portage around a short rapids.

When we were still more than half a mile from the rapids we spotted what appeared to be a man standing in the stream.

A stone man

The figure did not move, but looked more like a man the closer we approached. It was a disturbing, eerie sight, this motionless apparition awaiting us in a land where we expected to meet no one. Perhaps it was only a hallucination, a product of our fears and odd reflections off the water. Not until we were within a hundred yards of this lifelike figure did we see that it was stones piled one upon the other to resemble a man. It was built by the Indians, perhaps not so much to mark the way as to provide solace and reassurance—an indication that men had passed that way and that the land was not so destitute of life as it seemed. It might have been erected last year, or a century ago. It was nothing but a crude, faceless image of humanity, but for the traveler it was a guard against loneliness, and a link with the world of living men.

The area had often been camped in by the Indians, but it was still attractive because of the rapids, so we called it quits for the day.

Detritus

The most common objects in the trash scattered about those well-used campsites were lard cans—Burns lard, as a rule. Why Burns was the favorite is a mystery; perhaps it was cheaper, or maybe it was the bright red can. Baking powder containers were a close second to lard cans, followed by tobacco tins. Lard and baking powder, plus flour, salt, sugar, tea, and dried beans, are the staples of the Indians and other northern travelers. Supplemented by fish and game, these provide a nourishing if monotonous diet.

The portage route had been in use for generations. The Indians laid birch boughs over the rocks to ease the passage of their sleds in times of light snow.

John headed for the foot of the rapids, and on his first cast pulled out a jackfish. The fish were biting at anything that came their way. The jackfish, or northern pike as it's called in the United States, is scorned by many self-professed gourmets, but John and I thought it delicious. We suspected that its evil reputation was due to its ugly and ferocious appearance rather than a bad taste. It tasted much like trout, or like any freshwater fish—bland and requiring considerable seasoning.

Ugly as sin, but okay

Having not portaged that day, I thought I would feel more like portaging the next. Yesterday's pains were soon forgotten. We retained only a hazy, two-dimensional mental image; the physical reality was kindly omitted. Were it not so, we could scarcely have gone on. Had the memory of the Chipman portage—with its occasional rain, muskeg, aching muscles, raw feet, with its endless plodding forward under heavy loads in an atmosphere of misery and increasing despair—stayed with us for long, we would have been unable to face the prospect of portaging again. Fortunately, we were blessed with short memories. The immediate present intervened and obliterated the past.

Blessed amnesia

Another affliction hit us in the evening, something I had not been warned about. The no-see-ems arrived on the scene. They are aptly named. At first I thought I was being peppered by windblown grains of sand, but with my customary acuity I deduced that that couldn't be the case because the wind wasn't blowing. No-see-ems are gnatlike beasts that, thus far, did not seem inclined to bite or even to land on us. Their sole delight was in getting a good running start, hitting us in the face, bouncing off, and then having another go at it. No-see-ems did not engage in individual forays; they always attacked en masse. If their aim was annoyance they were highly successful. In waving futilely at them I often wound up hitting myself in the face.

We consistently turned in about midnight, since the bright glowing sky of extended twilight continued to deceive us into thinking it was earlier than it really was. Evening was the best time of day. With our chores done we were free to read or talk or—best of all—do nothing while enjoying the slowly changing colors in the sky, the sparkle of water, the dark serenity of the forest all around. Never was I more alert to beauty, more in harmony with myself and the world, or more alive, than when I was doing nothing.

Little-Stick Country

June 17

WE HAD OUR STANDARD BREAKFAST of oatmeal, fruit, and tea. Oatmeal was a fine, filling dish; its only drawback was that it required large amounts of sugar to make it palatable. We began the trip with nine pounds of sugar, but at the rapid rate we were consuming it we doubted that it would last—or rather, *I* doubted that it would last. John shrugged off my requests that he go easy on the sugar supply by simply repeating over and over that he was certain we had enough. I demonstrated mathematically that we would not have enough at the present rate of consumption, but John countered this by saying that he would rather use all the sugar he wanted then and have none at all later on, than to be partly satisfied all the time. And to show me that he meant it, he always took his customary eight to ten heaping teaspoons of the precious white stuff. John's notion was feast today and rely on blind optimism to take care of tomorrow, whereas I wanted to exercise willpower all the time so that we didn't eat ourselves into shortages of certain items long before the trip was over.

I found it strange that John and I should differ on such a matter. John was fully aware of the necessity for conserving our supplies and for being eternally watchful in all aspects of life and travel in the bush. The North is an unforgiving country; slight shortages and minor errors of judgment, normally of no consequence, tend to accumulate and can

Life is impulse

end in disaster. It was John, in fact, who frequently warned me of the dangers of carelessness, and dispensed advice on how to proceed. Sound advice it was, too, but John himself often was less able to take it to heart than I. He knew what was right, wise, and safe, but his is a restless and impatient nature. On occasion he answered questions by ignoring them, and surrendered to the impulse to put his head down and charge.

We began the day by wrestling everything across the three-chain portage, then loaded up and paddled three-fourths of a mile to the end of Chipman Lake. Off we went on a fifty-chain portage past a long and turbulent rapids. After the first carry we had our customary lunch of bread, jam, and cheese. We started on the last loaf of our store-bought bread, and soon John would have to demonstrate his skill at baking. Swarms of no-see-ems encouraged us to race through lunch and get on with the portaging. That done, we had a five-minute paddle followed by a twelve-chain portage, and we were on Bompas Lake. We saddled up again, made four or five miles, and camped for the night.

We had seen no game. The only mammal we had encountered was a voracious lemming who got into our food the fourth night out. It broke open several packages of Dri Lite but didn't eat much; apparently dehydrated foods were not to its liking. The animal got most of its nourishment from chewing one of my sneakers. We saw many ducks every day, usually in pairs since this was the mating season. In the evening the loons cried—a distinctly human sound, like a lost child calling out in fright. It was wild and lonely and haunting, perfect counterpart to the splash of water on the shore and the muted sigh of wind through the forest.

June 18

THE TRIP certainly was going as smoothly as could be expected. Our gear was finally organized and our routine established. Apparently we had remembered to bring everything, and we were getting along well together. Other than the unremitting hard labor, our only vexations were minor ones. For instance, my pen and pencil were covered with a gummy amalgam of sugar, dirt, and insect repellent. The repellent had remarkable properties: it discouraged the buggers and also dissolved paint and some kinds of plastic. I hated to think what it was doing to our skin. There had been no chance to bathe, for the water was much too cold. We were both somewhat rank, but didn't notice each other over our own stenches.

A large island—a "kame"—in Bompas Lake, bearing the last traces of winter.

We bless the map-makers

We had perfect weather, warm and completely clear all day long. What little wind we had was at our backs. It was a canoeists' paradise, except that the map messed us up twice. The first time was when we had a choice of passages past a mile-and-a-half-long island. We chose the narrower one because it was more sheltered. The map indicated that it went through, with minimum width of about a tenth of a mile. When we were three-fourths of the way through we ran out of water altogether. There was a hundred-foot-wide isthmus with a well-defined trail across it, and not the least trace of a channel. We dragged everything across the isthmus, cursing and fuming at the government cartographer who had made such an egregious mistake, although John finally felt compelled to make excuses for the anonymous bureaucrat.

Later, when we were looking for the portage to Selwyn Lake, we paddled up through one mild rapids, dragged the canoe up a second, and waded it up a third, only to find that the map was wrong again, or outdated. After we spent half an hour futilely casting about in what should have been the correct place, John had a brainstorm, walked cross-country to the east, and found the portage. It actually started directly from Bompas Lake, east of the first rapids. Rather than portage through thick bush, we ran back down the three rapids to the lake and hit the portage at its beginning. The portage was nearly three-quarters of a mile long and left us worn and weary, but we had to load up and set out onto the lake because there was not a good camping spot.

We paddled two and a half miles and finally landed at nine o'clock, too tired to go any farther. It was a tough place to unload: we had to thread the canoe through rock-studded shallow water and haul our gear up a four-foot bank. What was miserable work when we were fresh was doubly so when we were tired. I whipped up a quick meal of soup, spanish rice, peas, and pudding.

It was cold and clear when we hit the sack at midnight.

June 19

A FINE SUMMER DAY; it would have passed muster anywhere. We were still getting up late because we were turning in late. We started at 11:00, with nothing ahead of us for the day but paddling north and northeast on Selwyn Lake. At lunch we ate the last of the bread. Once we had finished it off it seemed like a luxury, even though it had become dry and stale.

Reverie

For two hours during early afternoon the lake was dead calm. Fluffy white clouds were scattered across a pastel blue sky. The air was hazy, both overhead and on the horizon. We were in a large, nearly circular portion of the lake, with land visible in all directions although there were channels north and south. Small forested islands seemed to be clumps of stone trees planted stiffly in a sheet of polished glass. Our paddles rose and fell, the canoe skated across that pure, gleaming surface, yet we got neither nearer to nor farther from any shore. The surface of the lake looked hard and thin, and beneath it was a dark void of unknown depth. We were suspended, perilously, on that fragile, brittle plane, struggling mightily to move forward but condemned to immobility in spite of all our efforts. Halfway between a warm, serene sky and a cold, watery bottom, equidistant from all shores, pawing at the water with flat pieces of wood. . . . There was not a breath of wind. We paddled on as in a dream, each of us lost in his own fantasies.

"The surface of the lake looked hard and thin . . . a dark void of unknown depth. We paddled on as in a dream . . . ."

Late in the afternoon the wind came up, and we had considerable hard paddling through waves before we landed on a narrow, short strip of gravel and sand beach. We made approximately twenty-two miles and were now in the Northwest Territories, half a mile north of the sixtieth parallel. John was most pleased, since he wanted to be at least that far north before the solstice.

Latitude 60

It had been a matter of some contention between us. John had been obsessed with the idea of achieving this arbitrary goal, and we drove ourselves hard to attain it. I felt strongly that the major reason for making the trip was for the sheer pleasure of being there, and that to turn the trip into a race or endurance contest was absurd and ruinous. We had had several arguments about it, and John promised that if I would indulge him in this one desire the trip would become more leisurely after we passed latitude sixty. It was now one week since we had last seen anyone—the Indians at the beginning of the Chipman portage. The only indication of other human life was the sound of a high-flying jet, too high to be seen.

On a low knoll 200 feet from where we pitched our tent were four Indian graves, one of them a child's. They were of indeterminate age, although we guessed they were at least

The Indian graves were several decades old, on a knoll overlooking the lake.

At the graves

twenty-five years old. All the graves were marked in the same way, with uprights at the four corners joined by horizontal slats two or three feet above the ground. The uprights on one were carved in the shape of spears. The markers were well weathered, and on one grave had partly collapsed. A third grave had a four-inch-high metal crucifix on it. All the Indians are now nominal Christians, either Anglican or Roman Catholic—with strong pagan overtones, John said. But most are certainly no more than nominally Christian. How can they be otherwise? Christianity is an alien religion, imposed from without and having no foundation in their own traditions, cultural life, and racial experience.

By late evening the lake was calm again. There was a lovely view to the southeast from the knoll near the graves. The water perfectly reflected a sky spotted with soft orange and pink clouds. The dark forest across the lake glowed red in the sunset. Thin black and green shadows leaped from shore and strained across the water like the outstretched arms of sleepwalkers. The silence and the extreme angle of the sun's rays accentuated the sense of vast distance and a loneliness of unbearable intensity. In that place, for those few moments, I felt that time and space and life were infinitely extended.

No beginning, no end

It was not entirely a pleasant feeling. A man wants to believe that there are limits somewhere, and the idea that in the realms of time and space there is possibly neither beginning nor end is a difficult thing to swallow. But swallow it or no, this journey was being made—or should have been—without reference to rigid, cherished beliefs. We were progressing northward geographically, but if we could rid ourselves of inhibiting ideas and stereotyped ways of regarding our surroundings and ourselves in them, then perhaps we could make a psychic journey backward toward origins and forward to a clearer vision of the future.

While I inspected the graves and meditated, John was engaged in more practical matters. He snagged a five-pound trout, and we polished it off for dinner. While we ate, two loons cavorted a hundred yards off shore. At times they appeared to be playing hide and seek. They both dived, staying submerged for a minute or two. The first one to surface turned its head this way and that, trying to anticipate where the other would rise. As soon as the second showed its head, the first went down again. The object of the game seemed to be to swim underwater and fool one's partner by coming up in an unexpected spot.

June 20

ANOTHER DAY of good weather. We had a tailwind in the morning and went scooting right along, but even with map and compass it was often difficult to be certain where we were. John fastened the map to a metal clipboard, and for easy reference tied it to the bag he was straddling. We both wore compasses around our necks, and occasionally John asked me to give him a heading or to take bearing on a point or island.

Selwyn Lake went on and on. It had a very irregular shoreline, and was dotted with small islands. Most of the islands were round, or nearly so. They were "kames," the result of debris falling into depressions in the glaciers. When the glaciers melted, the debris was deposited as mounds or ridges. Some of the lower islands—barely two or three feet above the water—had never developed any growth, and were nothing more than barren heaps of boulders. They were used as rookeries by herring gulls and Arctic terns, who rose up in alarm with much screeching when we approached too closely. The more aggressive gulls made dive-bombing runs on us, but scored no hits. The terns were the most fearless birds we had ever seen. They did not hesitate to attack the much larger gulls who encroached upon their territory. We found a terns' nest when we stopped for lunch, and it took both of us to get close enough for pictures—one to operate the camera and the other to shout and wave his arms at the terns as they dived at our heads.

Bombers and tough terns

After lunch the wind picked up and the water roughened. With our heavy load we had to head into the waves to keep from being swamped, which frequently had us paddling west when we wanted to go north and north-northeast. At four o'clock we gave it up as a bad job, and landed to lounge about and wait out the wind. A four-mile open stretch of lake lay ahead; we needed calm water with no threat of bad weather before we would attempt it.

John tried fishing but with no luck; the water was too rough. His pole broke again, and he gave up in disgust. The maxim of "the wind dies down at sundown" proved itself once again. We decided to eat and then try to cover some more miles afterward. As fast as we could prepare a dinner of soup, ham and beans, carrots, and pudding, we gulped it down. We started out again at eight o'clock and made about three miles, but we had to stop on the last island because of rough water—much too rough to attempt four miles of open crossing.

The wind dies down . . .

The island was a bad spot for camping: rough, rocky ground and swarming with mosquitoes. We had a very tough landing through shallow water, over slippery rocks, and up a bank through thick brush. We resolved to get up early in the morning and cross the open water before the wind rose, but midnight found us still sitting by the fire and talking.

June 21

THE LONGEST DAY of the year. We crossed the open stretch; it was a bit choppy but easily managed. We reached the portage to Flett Lake in early afternoon with a strong wind at our backs and the lake kicking up. Those big lakes were treacherous; they could blow up rough water from any direction on very short notice. We had a difficult landing, with waves smashing in and threatening to slam our canoe against some large boulders.

Looking south on Selwyn Lake, from the portage to Flett Lake.

Across the divide

Flett Lake is one hundred feet lower than Selwyn Lake. Selwyn, and all the water we had been on before it, drains to Lake Athabasca, Great Slave Lake, and down the Mackenzie River to the Arctic Ocean. Flett Lake drains to the northeast, down the Dubawnt and Thelon rivers to Chesterfield Inlet and Hudson Bay. There was a long portage, about a mile and a half, across the height of land separating the two watersheds. There was no muskeg, and we came to an occasional waist-high boulder on which we could set our loads and take a breather. Although we didn't know what we would encounter on our way up the Dubawnt River, John said that this was our last marked, established portage. From now on we would have to make our own, but we would be in terrain where the trees were thin and short—little-stick country—and we didn't expect any trouble.

The afternoon was hot, the forest tinder-dry and ripe for a fire, and we became quite parched. John took his camera with him on one carry and snapped a few pictures, but I wasn't able to work up any enthusiasm for such a task.

I feared that potentially the best pictures of the entire trip would never be taken. All the most dramatic moments would be lost, since both of us would be too busily engaged in creating the drama to record it for posterity. Once again I noted the need for a couple of healthy, hefty squaws, preferably registered nurses with a background in amateur photography.

Indian sign

We finished the portage to Flett Lake at six o'clock. At the end of every portage there was invariably a much-used Indian campsite, looking as though it had been frequented by a mob of sloppy tourists. Trees had been chopped and mutilated, scraps of paper and abandoned equipment were lying about, and there was plenty of "Indian sign"—several generations of dog droppings. There was everything one might find at a roadside rest, except beer cans and watermelon rinds. So although we were thoroughly worn and feeling quite weak, we put the canoe in the water and started out in search of a cleaner spot. We were soon attacked by a strong wind and the largest waves we had had the misfortune to be in. Even with both of us paddling strongly on the same side, the force of the wind almost turned us broadside on several occasions. After an anxious ten minutes we reached the lee of a small island, landed on it, and unloaded.

Summer solstice

How wearying the loading and unloading had become. It was a Sisyphean task; no matter how often we did it, it still must be done again. But soup and a Dri Lite meal revived us somewhat. As a solstice specialty I served eggnog—two cups apiece—one of the few luxury items we brought. Late in the evening we took some pictures and wandered around the higher and more open half of the island. I thought it hardly likely that anyone would ever have stopped on such an insignificant island before, but we found the ashes of two old fires. It had been the same everywhere; we had not yet found a place so remote that it hadn't been visited.

The sun set behind a ridge at 10:30. At the same moment a full moon rose in the opposite direction and gleamed white and cold on the water. There was a storm front moving in from the north—an exceedingly black sky with towering thunderheads. We made sure that both the tent and fly were securely fastened, and turned in after midnight.

June 22

A STIFF WIND blew all night, and the sky was solidly overcast in the morning. Just the sound of the wind was enough to tell us that the water was too rough. There was nowhere to go, so we lazily stayed in the sack until 10:30. Much of the day was spent reading, sharpening axes, and performing other household tasks. I applied waterproofing to my boots, and John shaved. The shave was a gory affair. True to his stoic philosophy John ripped away at his face and neck with the cheapest and dullest blade on the market, using only hand soap as a lubricant.

A moment of heightened pleasure. Author tending a bannock while relaxing with a good book.

John had been making bannock since our bread supply ran out. The recipe was one cup of flour, a teaspoon of baking powder, a teaspoon of salt, and just enough water to make a doughy paste. It was cooked by a combination of baking, frying, and a general exposure to hot coals. It could be done in a variety of ways, but usually John made a round flat cake out of the dough and placed it in a lightly greased frying pan. He put the pan on the grill over the fire for a few minutes to get the bottom done, then stood it close to the fire in a nearly vertical position with the handle supported by a stick. He rotated the bannock to get it done evenly, and in half an hour came up with the finished product, a heavy, dense, but eminently edible form of bread. It was very tasty, and a little went a long way, but it was too simple and easy a form of baking to suit John. He had ambitions to do bigger things, and wanted to bake real bread. But even after turning everything inside out we couldn't find the yeast. It spoiled his entire day. Of course, we would not have more food with bread rather than bannock, but the dough would rise more with yeast and give the illusion of more food.

It was cold and windy all day—never a chance to get moving. A dull, idle day, though not a complete waste; we needed the rest. Our concerns had become food, weather, distance traveled, and elementary physical comforts. Many of our conversations were about the benefits and afflictions of civilized existence, yet all of that was becoming increasingly ridiculous. Life as we still dreamed it no longer existed. Perhaps it never did.

Life is but a dream

For half an hour a ringed plover, digging up its evening meal, hopped across the mud and wet sand at the lake's edge. It was methodical, persistent, and quite unafraid of me as long as I did not move. Eventually it came right up to my feet, investigated the eyelets on my boots, and returned to the better nourishment in the mud.

Ringed plover. The smaller the bird, the less the fear.

Nomads

June 23

SOLID OVERCAST in the morning except for a streak of light far to the north. We quickly packed, and gladly left our little island. The lake was fairly calm to start with but roughened shortly after we set out. An intermittent drizzle began the moment we left. It never developed into a steady rain, but with the wind was enough to make it a damp, chilly, miserable day.

Another example of inadequate gear cropped up. My cheap plastic raincoat, all right for street wear, was unable to withstand any stress. Three hours of paddling nearly tore off one sleeve. We ran into big waves in the half hour before lunch, and had to tack easterly when we wanted to run north.

Angry words

John and I had a brief but angry exchange of words over whether we should continue to fight the wind and waves. I threw in his face his own remarks about exercising caution. He said that we would never get anywhere if we cringed on shore all the time. We glared at each other for a few moments, then calmed down, made apologetic noises, and continued with caution.

Our route took us on the lee side of a two-mile-long island. There was quite a stretch of open water ahead so we decided to stop for the day. The island marked the beginning of the transition zone between forested land and that of the Barrens.

Above a sandy beach was a ten-foot bluff of peat or compacted mosses. The terrain over an area the size of two football fields was devoid of trees. The ground was uneven and spongy, the first example of tundra we had seen. It supported mosses, sedges, and wildflowers, and presented a desolate aspect even in such a small patch.

Steady work, low wages

Although we made but six miles, I regarded the day as one of distinct attainment. In this age of the division of labor there are few men who, upon finishing a day's work, understand how the product of their effort fits into a larger context—or makes any sense at all. Did traveling six miles by canoe make sense? Of course it did! It concentrated our efforts and lent purpose to our lives. We were made whole by the knowledge that we had not committed a phantom deed.

June 24

ANOTHER GRAY overcast day. Very strange weather; always threatening a storm, but never raining. It was windy and cold on exposed portions of the lake but comfortable when we were in narrow channels or to the lee of one of the numerous islands. It was often difficult to find the way when looking at such a maze of islands from water level and comparing it with a map scaled four miles to the inch. In midafternoon we crossed from Flett Lake to Wholdaia Lake. The change was marked by a shallow channel a hundred yards wide with many boulders protruding above the surface, and a barely noticeable current.

A short time later we came upon a black bear, the first specimen of large mammal life we had seen. He was lying on the shore in a dazed state. We paddled quietly to within a hundred feet of him before he spotted us and regarded us with bland curiosity. The wind was not right for him to get our scent, and he seemed neither alarmed nor angered. I took

Bear photos

several pictures, but when John readied his camera the bear ambled off into the bush. We shouted and whistled, and he stuck his head out to see what all the commotion was. More noise from us brought him back to shore, and we finished with our photography. He was a very willing subject, with a beautiful glossy coat and a somewhat bewildered expression. When he walked he resembled two clumsy boys dressed in a bear suit.

Posing

We had an excellent fish dinner, courtesy of John. Also rice, chicken gravy, green beans, and lemon pudding as my contribution. As I frequently remarked to John, our meals were more elaborate, and I was doing far more cooking, than when I had the advantage of a modern kitchen. Back in civilization we used to throw together a quick meal from whatever was in the refrigerator or cupboard, wolf it down, and run off to what we thought was more important. But now that we were far from all that feverish activity, dinner had become a significant event, and we did it up brown every night.

We had guests for dinner: mosquitoes by the billion. They were the most aggressive and headstrong in their approach to nourishment I had ever met. They flew into my eyes, and when I opened my mouth they flew down my throat. They flew into the food and expired, both while it was cooking and while on our plates. I splashed some insect repellent into my hand preparatory to rubbing it on my face and neck. At that very moment a mosquito dived into the blob of liquid, struggled for an instant, and died. Not smart enough to be repelled, he drowned. *Sic transit gloria mundi.*

Strong mosquitoes

We made seventeen miles.

June 25

OUR FOURTH CONSECUTIVE DAY of somber weather. The sky was solidly overcast but there was still no rain. We got off to our usual late start, but the trip was, after all, a vacation and not a race. Ideally we should have lived by the sun and paid no heed to the hands of our watches, but the habit of regulating our lives by clocks was too strong. Although we certainly had developed some slothful habits, we were making good time and had no need to worry on that score. Our only deadline was Snowdrift by approximately August 25. After that we would run the risk of cold weather, which is both uncomfortable and dangerous. Moffatt, who was farther north than we would be and in the Barrens as well, died of hypothermia on September 14 with the air temperature at twenty degrees. After his canoe overturned in a rapids he was in the water for twenty or thirty minutes, and the combination of shock and exposure did him in.

We had a tailwind most of the morning, and no large waves. But the gloomy weather left both of us a bit depressed and longing to see the sun again. Water and sky and land blended into a dull, lusterless monochrome. The whole world, from the lake's surface to the horizon and up to the zenith, was a lifeless gray, the way the earth will look in that distant eon when the sun is cooling and the planet becomes moribund and turns to ice.

Indians' canoe cached on an island in Wholdaia Lake.

It was calm in the afternoon as we crossed a four-mile stretch of open water, headed due north. Wholdaia Lake was huge, strewn with islands and abounding in coves and bays. It must have been a great puzzle to those who went that way before it was mapped. Samuel Hearne crossed Wholdaia Lake on the ice in February 1771 on his way from Prince of Wales Fort (present-day Churchill, Manitoba) on Hudson Bay to the mouth of the Coppermine River on Coronation Gulf. He recrossed the lake on his return journey in May 1772. Hearne's travels are one of the most remarkable feats in the annals of exploration. In two and a half years he walked close to 5,000 miles through some of the least hospitable territory on earth, accompanied only by Indians who were often hostile and loath to lead him farther. Some of the areas he explored are so remote and have such a fierce climate that they were not revisited by white men until this century.

An empty country

The only change since Hearne passed this way is that the country is now entirely uninhabited. The bands of nomadic Indians no longer exist. It is estimated that the present population of northern Indians is one-tenth of what it was 200 years ago. Their ranks have been decimated by smallpox, tuberculosis, diphtheria, and starvation. Those remaining now cluster around the trading posts, if possible working for wages in summer, and in winter going into the bush to trap for furs. They no longer roam as far or as long as they once did.

We were the nomads now—made seventeen miles again.

June 26

WE WERE actually out of the sack by 8:00 and under way by 9:45. Of course the sun had been up for a good six hours, so we were only relatively early. We made about eight miles before stopping for lunch on a miraculously bug-free island.

We had the last long stretch of Wholdaia Lake to cross, about ten miles due north. The wind and weather were too erratic for such a long open crossing, so we followed the eastern shore until increasing waves forced us to head in at three o'clock. We spent an hour and a half lying on a sandy beach in warm sunshine, alternately talking and snoozing.

A life of leisure

I looked up at the blue sky and white clouds, listened to the waves splashing ashore at my feet, felt the sun on my face, and imagined that I was leading a life of leisure on a remote Caribbean island.

When the waves didn't go down, we paddled along close to shore for a quarter of a mile and camped on a sandspit. The country had become more open, and we spotted good campsites in abundance. We had made about eleven miles. It wasn't spectacular progress, but three hours of calm water would put us into Anaunethad Lake, the last lake before we headed up the Dubawnt River. It was now two weeks since we had seen the Indians, and the odds were that we wouldn't see anyone else until we got to Snowdrift. We couldn't have asked for anything more.

June 27

THERE WERE several brief, heavy showers during the night. We remained snug and dry, and slept soundly through most of them. It was quite windy; the walls of the tent puffed in and out like a bellows.

Tied down by reality

The wind and waves kept us tied down in the morning. Strength, intelligence, ingenuity—none of those did any good when the wind blew. The weather improved by midday. We shoved off at one o'clock. During the afternoon we covered the remainder of Wholdaia Lake and camped on a sandy shore facing due west.

Often when we paddled across a long stretch of open water my mind became engrossed with trivia. That afternoon I determined that I took, on the average, twenty-five strokes per minute. Then I paddled two hours straight and never missed a beat—some 3,000 strokes. This modest show of endurance and determination gave me inordinate pride.

During the evening a duck landed in our cove, returning several times and coming closer on each occasion. We permitted it to live because we couldn't be bothered with it at the time, but we definitely were thinking of having a duck dinner in the near future.

Unreality

Although John and I had much in common, he differed sufficiently from me that I wished I knew better what made him tick. That evening I brashly intimated that I had some insight into his subconscious, and at once we plunged into a long, avid, but not very coherent discussion of psychoanalysis, which John mistrusted because it is not a science with rigid laws and formulas, a science whose theses and theories can be demonstrated as "facts" by conducting experiments that any logical person can follow and admit are correct. John said he was a determinist, right down the line. I was shocked! All this made for interesting talk, although at times it deteriorated to the level of "how many angels can dance on the head of a pin?" There was much proselytizing, but no converts were made.

Reality

The sun went down at 10:30 bearing 330 degrees true. Immediately after sunset the clouds were shades of red and orange and violet. Though the sun was below the horizon for four or five hours, there was no total darkness—merely a period of suffused glow during which lingering red twilight faded slowly into pale dawn.

June 28

IT WAS A MISERABLE DAY—solidly overcast, sporadic rain, strong wind, and many whitecaps in the direction we wished to go. The water was much too rough for traveling.

The rover boys in the bush

We managed to get a fire going by liberally dousing some twigs with lighter fluid. I twitted John about using a civilized aid such as the fluid while on what was supposed to be a great wilderness experience. He squelched me by replying that the object was not to demonstrate our Boy Scout skills, but rather to get a fire started in the quickest and easiest fashion. How right he was, although actually the question remained as to where to draw the line. If we had applied John's reasoning cross the board we would have used a kicker rather than paddles, had our food airlifted to us weekly rather than carried it, or—easier yet—we would have stayed home.

Heavy work

After breakfast I retired to the tent, and John soon followed. I began reading *Mao-tse Tung: An Anthology of His Writings* by Anne Fremantle, and later in the day switched to *Gabriela, Clove and Cinnamon* by Jorge Amado. John tried to read *The Cannibal* by John Hawkes, but didn't care for it because of "surrealism" and "it takes too much effort." Our cold hands clutched the books, there was an incessant patter of rain on our canvas roof, and it was indeed difficult to concentrate. John took a crack at *Unpopular Essays* by Bertrand Russell, but couldn't make a go of that either. He started on Céline's *Journey to the End of the Night*, which he found more to his liking. I hoped that wasn't a prophetic title.

The weather gradually worsened. We had lunch huddled inside the tent. Every so often one of us went out to heap wood on the fire, and when it was again blazing returned to the tent. When the fire was reduced to embers we repeated the process and thus kept it going all day, even through periods of downpour.

We felt quite pent up in our small tent, and very cold. We were prisoners: the only alternative to being trapped in the tent was to be outside getting wet. For the first time I thoroughly missed the amenities of civilized existence: the comforts, the entertainments, and especially the numerous sources of intellectual stimulation.

Yet that civilized life had ceased to exist for us, except as an abstraction—albeit one that provided us with many topics of conversation. We avidly discussed politics; fortunately we had the same political orientation. And we wondered what was going on in that madcap world to the south of us. (John referred to anywhere south of wherever we happened to be at the moment as "The Banana Belt.") We wouldn't know anything about current events until late August or early September, by which time many contemporary concerns would be ancient history. The country would be worrying about, and ignoring, new crises, issues, names, personalities—"all that blah, blah, blah," said John. Events whip by on a conveyor belt these days—or is it a squirrel cage?

Banana Belt madness

June 29

INTERMITTENT RAIN fell all night and on into the morning. There was still an overcast when we arose, but it soon lifted somewhat and started breaking up to the north. It took us the better part of an hour to get a fire going with wet wood.

John shaved again, but I decided to let my beard grow for the entire trip. I was over the bristly, uncomfortable stage, and simply couldn't be bothered. Also I found that a beard was great protection against insects and cold.

The weather improved, and we got the show on the road at 2:30. It was a nice day for traveling, except that parts of

The two-room cabin had been built by experienced hands.

There's nothing like corrugated cardboard to keep out the wind.

Anaunethad Lake, a half mile or more from land, were infested with gnats, migrating hither and yon in swarms. They didn't bite, but made a damned nuisance of themselves by plowing into our eyes, ears, nostrils, mouths, and hair.

A canoeist paddles on his stomach

We made eight miles and stopped to camp at 5:30. After dinner we had a fine talk about food. Would our supplies last? How would our meals be revised when we ran out of various items? What would we do differently if we had the opportunity to buy provisions for such a trip again? And then we got off onto more esoteric aspects of food, such as Paris restaurants we'd enjoyed and classic meals we'd eaten or dreamed of eating. Food was now a major interest and prime topic of conversation. As our lives became more primitive—in the sense that we were more concerned with essentials—food undoubtedly would take on still greater importance and interest than it already had.

A hundred feet back from the lake was a sturdy cabin. It looked as though it had been occupied within the past year or two, probably by an Indian family. Inside were several pieces of homemade furniture, an oil-drum stove, tins of baking powder, peanut butter, and Player's cigarettes, and two pairs of children's shoes hanging from a rafter.

There was a light local shower. The sun was low on the horizon, shining through scattered clouds and sparkling on raindrops falling in the lake. There were four small islands about a hundred yards from shore. They looked black, cold, lonely, sinister. It was the Far North as one romantically imagined it should look, but it left me with a sense of foreboding. Perhaps John and I should have erected our own stone men so that we would have something to look back upon as we paddled farther into the wilderness.

"... black, cold, lonely, sinister." The Far North as one imagines it.

Up the Dubawnt

June 30

WE BUCKED A BRISK WIND as we headed across the last two miles of Anaunethad Lake. With our load, we were not able to make more than a mile and a half or two miles an hour. We were glad to be getting off the big lakes. River travel would be a novelty—a pleasant one we hoped.

Although we hadn't seen anyone since the Chipman portage, we were now getting into an even less populated land. The Indians apparently don't go that way any more, so it is only the rare voyageurs such as ourselves who go over that route. We didn't know how many white men had gone before us on that portion of the Dubawnt River. Blanchet came downriver in 1917; to our knowledge, he was the only one who had done so and written about it. One thing we knew for certain: there would be no established portages.

Off the beaten path

We started up the river. With strenuous paddling we covered about a quarter of a mile against a moderate current, then hauled the canoe, both of us knee-deep to waist-deep in the stream, about 100 yards farther to the foot of half a dozen three-foot-high shelves. There we had lunch, then portaged around the white water, about a fifth of a mile. For the first hundred yards it was rough going through swamp and low-branching trees. The remainder was easy walking over an esker, a long, narrow deposit of sand and gravel left by a river flowing through or under a glacier during the ice age. Some eskers meander across the countryside for many miles, disappearing in present-day lakes and streams but reappearing as islands or ridges. We sought out eskers for overnight stops, since they invariably provided easy landing, good campsites, and plenty of fuel. The porous soil of eskers grows larger trees, although fewer of them, than does lower, flatter land.

Paddling uphill

The loading was the worst yet. We had to cross a strip of jumbled boulders with our loads and put them in the canoe while standing in shallow water with very slippery rocks underfoot. We paddled for five minutes across a wide calm spot in the river, then struggled up through 150 feet of swift current. It was almost too much for us, but all-out, desperate paddling got us through an inch at a time. It took three minutes at fifty strokes to the minute (twice our normal rhythm), every muscle straining and the paddles bending as we ripped them through the water. After that we had an easy two-mile paddle across an unnamed lake to the foot of the rapids leading to Smalltree Lake. We found easy walking on the north bank of the river around a ladder-type rapids about a quarter-mile long. We did half the portage to a good camping spot, and would start the morning with the remaining half—to be followed by a stint of wading and other such pleasures.

The Dubawnt River between Anaunethad Lake and Smalltree Lake. An easy river to go down, but going up meant two days of hard work to cover eight miles.

John had an aerial photograph of that portion of the route, but it covered just to the head of the rapids that we could see from our campsite. At that point the river made a bend, and the map was not sufficiently detailed to give us a clue as to what we could expect. The river was supposed to rise eighty-six feet between Anaunethad Lake and Smalltree Lake, but neither of us could judge very well how much altitude we had gained by passing through or around the various rapids. No matter how high we had risen, though, it had been exhausting work, with our boots and pants wet for hours at a time.

The choice: Stoic, or Insane

We were less than fifty miles south of the Barrens. The trees were noticeably smaller than those on Wholdaia Lake and southward. The no-see-ems were very bad, coming in swarms and undaunted by repellent. John said that after a few months in the North one becomes either stoic or insane. It sounded true. I had worn a headnet the past two evenings. It was a nuisance, but soothed the nerves and permitted me to think about something other than annihilating the insects.

July 1

EVERY DAY we made valiant resolutions, but only half-hearted efforts, to change our sleeping hours, develop good habits, and use our time more efficiently. But why? We felt no pressure of time, and did not need to do more than we were doing, or even to think in terms of efficiency.

We were off to an early start in good weather. There were only a few clouds, and the temperature was just right for a day of exertion. We finished off the remainder of the short portage we were on, feeling chipper at the prospect of getting up the Dubawnt River with such ease. We loaded the canoe, and after 200 yards of paddling came around a bend and beheld another stretch of white

Not so easy

water. We tried hauling the canoe up through it, but after only a hundred feet it became too shallow. There was nothing to do but wade back down to the foot of the rapids, land on the south

bank, and reconnoiter. John picked out a portage route about a quarter-mile long, through the edge of a stand of trees and in sight of the river all the way.

We ate lunch before portaging. Since we had expected to be on Smalltree Lake by midafternoon at the latest, we had not prepared a regular lunch. We made do with a quarter-pound of cheese and a chocolate bar apiece. With the benefit of hindsight it was easy to see that I erred badly in buying only fifty chocolate bars. This permitted us one apiece every third day, a regimen we had followed religiously. But because we had not prepared a lunch we cheated by one day and would have to wait four days for the next bar. This was all due to our blandly confident expectation of cruising up the Dubawnt with no trouble. Had we not been eternally alert, this was the sort of thing that could have been our downfall. Let this be a lesson to those who think that one should learn something from experience: the wages of optimism are destruction of principle, collapse of discipline, and moral breakdown—I told myself as I relished my chocolate bar a day early.

Moral collapse

Then we portaged, hoping that we had the river whipped. But a short paddle brought us to some more current, more wading, and eventually another portage. There was no trace of an established trail on any of these portages. We made our own routes by picking the likelier-looking bank—usually on the inside of a bend, if there was one—then went inland a few yards in search of the best walking conditions. The land on both sides of the river was thickly overgrown and poorly drained. In effect, there weren't any good walking conditions, merely some that weren't quite as bad as others. Most of the time we slogged through muskeg or crashed through underbrush. The portage seemed to be as much as half a mile long, although we were so weary we may have been overestimating distances.

While we were on the second carry, each of us with a box, I sank up to my knees in a patch of swamp, and in spite of frantic efforts to stay upright I lost my balance and toppled over on my side in six inches of spongy mud and black, stagnant water. I went down in such a way that I was unable to unstrap myself from the load or to get on my feet again. So I lay in the muck, muttering the foulest curses I could think of, until John put down his own box and came to my assistance. I was outraged and humiliated. I hated to be bested by the conspiracy of a dirty swamp and a box I had built myself.

Swamped

After that fiasco we got loaded up and on the water again, for even though it was past our normal stopping time we wanted to get to Smalltree Lake and find a good campsite. But after less than half a mile of paddling we were confronted by another rapids. We landed on the north side in a swampy, bug-infested place, and searched out a portage route about a quarter of a mile long. It wasn't such bad walking, considering what we had already been through, but we were much too tired to do it. We crossed to the south bank and went downstream a hundred yards to the only possible campsite we had seen, a sparsely wooded piece of high ground. The unloading was awkward and difficult. I stood on shore and John stood in the canoe, which was parallel to shore. With great effort we heaved the boxes and bags out of the canoe and up a steep bank. It was sometimes impossible to tell whether we were handling the baggage or it was throwing us around.

Camping

Everything took an inordinate length of time. We moved slowly and erratically because we were tired and had not eaten since early morning except for our meager lunch. I threw together a huge supper of soup, a double order of spanish rice, green beans, and fruit. It was 9:15 when we landed, and midnight when the dishes were washed. Our boots, socks, and pants were thoroughly soaked, and got only partly dry by the fire.

Supper

The no-see-ems were with us all day, and in the evening the mosquitoes joined in. They never let us alone for an instant, even when we were out on the water paddling. After an entire day of that sort of thing we were not only physically tired but emotionally exhausted. Constant attack by endless swarms of insects is extraordinarily hard on the nerves. After several hours of it I felt like screaming or crying or jumping into the water to seek relief. The trip was rapidly becoming a masochist's delight.

Bugs

July 2

By some miracle John was up at eight o'clock and off in the canoe to try his luck at fishing. I didn't get up until 9:30, when John returned with a twenty-nine-inch jackfish. Although we didn't feel up to par, we started right out. We were determined to do our resting at a choice spot on Smalltree Lake rather than on an insect-ridden piece of tundra. We made it over the portage, but with a noticeable lack of verve. Finally, though, we had the Dubawnt River beaten. The lake opened before us and we looked out on several miles of clear sailing—a blessed relief.

Author, just after landing on the island in Smalltree Lake. We felt "sort of listless."

All afternoon we bucked a headwind (the whole world was against us!), but at six o'clock we reached our preselected camping spot—on an island one and a half miles north by south and a half mile east by west, divided into two nearly equal parts that were joined by a narrow strip of sand. We had chosen this site from one of John's aerial photos; it looked ideal. The same thought had occurred to others—about half the sand strip was pretty well fouled up by what was once a base camp for the Geological Survey of Canada.

The ruins of our age

Bottles, tin cans, and much other debris littered the place. The camp dated from 1961, judging from a scrap of newspaper we found in the wreckage. There was a partly collapsed float-plane dock, and a dozen empty gasoline drums on the beach.

We moved up the strip and settled in an unspoiled spot on the east shore thirty feet from the water. Fifty feet behind us was the west shore. It was the same lake on both sides, but the two parts of it frequently presented different aspects. When we landed, the west had gently rolling waves and the east was placid. As the canoe nosed onto the beach, John remarked in a dull tone: "I feel sort of listless." A remarkable understatement; I was thoroughly bushed. That struggle coming up the Dubawnt took a lot out of us, but we expected to recuperate with ease. We were going to stay there for three or four days, and we intended to treat ourselves well.

For a starter I prepared a large evening meal, featuring—as an epicurean treat—a can of freeze-dried meatballs, with

Feasting

vegetable stew, fried potatoes, and pudding made with Klim (a brand of whole dry milk—milk spelled backward). Due to an unsurpassed lack of forethought we had brought only one small can, and until then had been making our puddings with water. It didn't harm their taste, but of course they wouldn't jell and we drank our puddings rather than ate them.

How pleasant it was that we didn't have to get up early in the morning. There would be nothing to do but take life easy.

July 3

I WAS AWAKENED at 4:00 by the sun shining in my eyes. At 7:00 we both arose, but only because it was too hot in the tent and the dive-bomber buzzing of deer flies was getting on our nerves. It was the first day that deer flies and black flies were out in large numbers. If it wasn't one plague it was another; we were expecting locusts any day.

As the first order of this lazy day John tried casting from the beach, and quickly snared a trout in three feet of water. It was fish enough for breakfast and lunch. For breakfast we also had bacon and eggs—quite a high-class meal. Later John baked biscuits, which we had for lunch; they were a delightful change from bannock.

Bathing bush babies

The temperature went above ninety degrees—Banana Belt weather. We plunged into the lake for our first bath since leaving Edmonton. The water was still shockingly cold, but it was wonderful to feel at least halfway clean again. Later we pored over the maps. We were roughly one-third of the way along on the trip, with—we hoped—most of the toughest portaging behind us.

In the evening after dinner we walked up onto the high part of the island, the southern end. The highest spot, about 300 feet above the lake, was a barren pile of shattered rocks from which we had a view of many miles in all directions. The island apparently was a huge kame, having within it half a dozen small serene ponds—"kettles." The shore of the largest pond was but twenty feet from the shore of Smalltree Lake, but there was no connection between the two. The northern half of the island was low and flat, half of it forested and the rest tundra. The south portion was almost entirely barren except in sheltered places on the lower slopes. There were several "strand lines," indicating former lake levels as the land has gradually risen since the melting of the glaciers. The highest line was about 200 feet above the present lake.

Kames, kettles, strand lines

A good breeze came up, and for the first time we were free of insects. Dark clouds were gathering to the north and west. Streaks of rain fell across a strip of incandescent orange sky as we returned to the tent. We battened down for the night and turned in, both of us confessing to great lethargy. The clouds were quite close, with thunder and lightning.

July 4

THERE WAS a light splatter of rain during the night, but by morning the clouds had blown away and it looked like another scorcher. The question of the day: Should we observe the Fourth of July in the Northwest Territories? The answer: no. We had no desire to engage in nationalist celebration, had no floats to parade nor armies to review nor missiles to count, and belonged to no civic or fraternal organizations. Nor did we have fireworks, which definitely put the kibosh on it.

After breakfast I headed for the high part of the island again to take some pictures, while John sought to deceive and snare a fish. As I left the beach and started up the slope I flushed a grouse. The fool bird, after the fashion of its stupid kind, ran along the ground in front of me for a short distance and then flew into a tree fifteen feet away. I returned to camp, got John and his .22, and we went back to where I'd seen the grouse. Sure enough, there he was, still sitting in the same tree. John knocked him off, and we roasted him under hot coals for lunch. Killing and eating a Canadian bird struck us as a fitting and proper way to mark an American holiday.

Patriotism

Actually we were never conscious of being in a country other than our own; or, more correctly, I should say that we were not conscious of being in *any* country. We were in a

The Fourth of July on Smalltree Lake. We camped on the narrow strip of land connecting the two parts of the island.

wilderness that had no national markings, and whatever part of it we were in we regarded as ours. We were at home in all latitudes.

As the latest defense against insects we put rubber bands around our pants cuffs; they kept the buggers from flying up our legs. Both of us had from thirty to fifty bites on each leg between ankle and knee. Apparently it was the no-see-ems who did the greatest damage; the fierce itching from their bites lasted several days. Often at night I was awakened by the itching, scratched madly until the blood flowed, then dropped off to sleep again.

They got us

As on any day after a strong wind, the lake was covered with a light green pollen. It was blown to us from all those unknown shores, lapping up and piling on the beach in sterile rows. Frequently as we plowed through the bush on a portage, our shirts and pants were streaked with this sweet pale dust.

After a Dri Lite supper, the wild-food department took a turn for the better. As I was walking to the abandoned survey camp for a load of the loose firewood there, I spotted a solitary duck floating benignly in our lake. John came hurrying with the .22 and got it through the neck at a distance of 200 feet. Later he pulled a twenty-eight-inch jackfish from the lake in front of the tent. Before he snagged the fish he also found the time and ambition to bake a raisin pie.

John got them

He did the baking in an improvised reflector oven. Using our rectangular grill as a base, he attached heavy wire to both ends and installed panels of aluminum foil on three sides. The pie sat on the open grill, and a roaring fire was built opposite the open side.

None of the effort required to construct makeshift arrangements of this sort was necessary. We could perfectly well have done without a reflector oven. But for John that sort of thing was an integral part of a wilderness experience, as were hunting, fishing, and canoeing itself. For him they were partly a means to an end, but mainly the expression of a need to demonstrate to himself that by a combination of skill and

ingenuity he could cope with the problems of life in the bush. In my view, those activities were not pleasurable at all; most of them were onerous tasks that must be performed if one was to get along. But I was most fortunate in having John as a traveling companion. Even though I had no desire to cultivate any of his skills, I was fully aware that the trip would have been harder and riskier had I made it with another greenhorn.

Perfect vision

Whereas John's forte was action, I tended more to contemplation. I lay on my back in the warm sand, hands behind my head, and basked in twilight's slowly changing colors. As I gazed across the lake to a distant shore I had one of those fleeting, lucid, impossible-to-capture moments of heightened awareness. For an instant I could see, and understand, my life—past, present, and projected into the future—the world, the universe, the entire scope and meaning of human history. In that moment of transcendent consciousness it all blended to form a coherent whole, a wonderfully complete and viable realm in which I could have lived happily forever. I held harmony and repose in my grasp. It was enough. I was content.

John, the thoughtful baker, tending a batch of biscuits in the makeshift reflector oven.

July 5

THE DAY was burning hot at 7:30. The air was still, the sky unblemished. The black flies buzzed around us at high speed, like Indians circling a beleaguered wagon train. The northern exaggeration has it that black flies don't merely bite, they tear off a hunk of meat and fly up into the trees to eat it while perched on a limb.

In the middle of the afternoon we went in swimming and bathing again. The water had warmed appreciably in the past two days, and was quite comfortable to a depth of two feet; we didn't go out much deeper than that anyway. We plunged in fully dressed and rinsed a little dirt out of the clothes we were wearing. Both of us had three sets of outer clothing, but we hoped to get along on two sets and save the clean ones for when we hit Yellowknife. A peculiarity of black flies was that they greatly preferred us wet. While we were in the water we had to keep moving and splashing, or submerged, and once ashore it was run for the fire, which dispersed them at once.

Reinvigorated

We would leave the island the next day, well fed, well rested, clean, and with all minor repairs made to clothing and equipment. One Woods bag had to be sewed at the seams for a couple of inches in each of four spots, but the boxes had held up wonderfully well in spite of the beating we had given them. In another two weeks we expected to be able to consolidate our gear and dispose of one box. It would give John leg room and enable us to balance the canoe better, and—especially—cut one carry off the portages.

A World to Ourselves

July 6

THIRTY MINUTES OF PADDLING landed us on the northwest shore of the lake. We had an air photo covering the area, and since there was no portage route we had to make our own. This was done by the simple expedient of drawing a line on the photo from our landing spot to the point we wished to hit on Andrecyk Lake, figuring the compass bearing—353 degrees true in this case—and following that bearing on as nearly a straight line as possible.

Canoeing on land

The first 300 yards were across tundra, through a bit of muskeg, and up a thirty-foot slope onto an esker. After that it was easy walking through a lightly forested area, nearly level and with good footing. Most of the portage was through this open-park country. It was sandy, and high enough so that it had drained well. The trees were taller than those close to lakes and rivers, and the only hindrance was the need to constantly take bearings. We sighted on an exceptionally tall tree, walked to the base of it, and took another bearing—about 200 feet at a crack. There was little underbrush, and it was easy to hold a course. Toward the end the terrain became gradually wetter and more thickly overgrown, until the final 200 yards which were very swampy. We leaped from one hummock to another, sinking into water and muck and crashing and blundering through intertwined tree limbs. The day was hazy and exceedingly sultry—hot and humid in a way reminiscent of the eastern United States at that

time of year. We perspired mightily, and the first carry left us feeling as though we had already done a hard day's work.

The portage was at least a mile and a half and took us more than two hours with a load, and the walk back to Smalltree Lake tired us further. On our second carry, both of us with our boxes and I leading the way, I somewhere veered to the right and we walked a half mile too far, missing the cove we were headed for and winding up on a different strip of beach altogether. The weather grew more oppressive as the afternoon wore on, and the black flies were merciless. They never let us alone, and became more numerous on the third carry when we were streaming sweat and making slow time. There was no way to combat them. Insect repellent was quickly washed away by sweat, and our hands were occupied with grasping a tumpline or shoulder straps. It made us appreciate the problem posed by insects to animals with inadequate tails and no other means of defense. There are stories of instances when caribou, in their frantic efforts to escape swarms of flies, rushed blindly off a cliff and fell to their deaths on the rocks below. Suicide was not our game, though; we gritted our teeth and kept going.

The flies were winning

John had the canoe for his third carry. Shortly after he started out, as he was stepping across a narrow rivulet at the base of the esker, he lost his footing and went into the water up to his buttocks with the canoe on top of him. The canoe fell with a hollow clunk, and then I heard John's cries of disgust and annoyance, sounding as though he was calling from an echo chamber. I turned around, but all I could see was the

Memories

canoe flat on the ground with John apparently underneath. He was unharmed, but the effort he made both in trying to stay upright and then in getting out from under and picking up the canoe again called for the sort of reserve strength that neither of us had.

In the final 200 yards of the third carry John and the canoe became jammed between two trees. I shouted to him to back up if he could, and that I would put down my load and return to help him. But one of those stubborn moments was upon him. Again and again he stepped back a few paces then lunged forward, until about the tenth try when he rammed his way through amidst a tremendous clanging of metal and splintering of branches. Sometimes, it would seem, the "charge" approach to life is the most effective.

Self-employed

We finished the portage shortly after 6:00, completely exhausted and with swarms of black flies driving us out of our minds. Blood was running down from behind John's ears, a favorite target area of the flies, and we certainly didn't feel as though we'd just had a three-day rest. We couldn't imagine doing that sort of a thing as a job; no one pays enough money to make it worthwhile.

It was remarkable how my state of mind could change during the course of a day; and even though I knew it was going to change under certain circumstances, I was powerless to control my attitudes and emotions. On a day such as that, when by late afternoon I was grinding along in a cloud of despair and getting no pleasure whatsoever out of life, I focused my feelings of annoyance and misery on John. I wanted to blame him for putting me in such a fix, although I was fully aware that I had gone up there of my own volition—quite eagerly, at that. I wanted to call John every name in the book, and wildly accuse him of an immense variety of crimes. I wanted to drop my pack, or lie down and quit, or make a beeline for the Banana Belt, or anything at all to escape from an intolerable state of affairs. Fortunately I neither did nor said anything, being always rational enough to realize that nothing would do any good. Sooner or later it would all be over, and within a few minutes of putting down the last load my feelings were reversed. Once more I appreciated the beauty around me, my attitude toward John was friendly, and I was able to laugh again. In half an hour everything looked rosy.

J'accuse

The sultry day turned into an evening of violent thunderstorms—short, heavy downpours accompanied by

The Gods look down

much lightning and noise. It was easy to understand how primitive people might interpret such phenomena as manifestations of the Rain God's anger. What other explanation could there possibly be?

July 7

VERY HAZY AGAIN in the morning, but the rain clouds had blown away and the lake was calm. We paddled for two hours, stopped for a lunch of beans and tea, paddled another two and a half hours, and our day was done. We were at the western end of Andrecyk Lake, having covered about fourteen miles.

The country was much more open. All ridges and areas exposed to the wind were bare of trees, and there was considerably less underbrush in the forests. It was more attractive that way than when entirely wooded. Some of the islands were perfectly contoured. Only a thin overlay of grass, mosses, lichens, and a few trees covered what was deposited by the glaciers.

The daylight hours already had grown perceptibly shorter, but not by enough to make us change our habits. At ten o'clock there were cloud streamers in the sky, and a soft light that seemed to emanate from all directions. John mixed bannock while I wrote my journal. The last six evenings had been still and warm—no wind, and scarcely a ripple on the water. Also no other people, and only about once a week the distant hum of an airplane engine.

Sins of the Banana Belt

In the afternoon while paddling lazily across the lake we discussed Castro's Cuba, the effects of the Cold War on the Western Hemisphere, and Latin American social, political, and economic problems. It was remarkable how vehement we became when debating the world's troubles, and laughable when I thought about such concerns and interests in the present context of our lives. We were paddling and portaging, north of the sixty-first parallel in the center of the wilderness on what apparently was a deserted planet, or, if inhabited, one whose ills and worries were so remote as to be of no import. And as the days drifted by, those concerns would recede still farther. We would traverse the northern lakes and forests forever, never returning to the lives we left behind.

Life is just egocentric

In reading over what I had just written I was surprised and amused to see the phrase "in the center of the wilderness." One's ego continued to function as foolishly as ever, and insisted on being at the center of something, much as ancient peoples postulated an Earth-centered universe. But to say "the center of the wilderness" was akin to saying "the center of a vacuum." Whether we were at the center or on the fringe of the wilderness was irrelevant. Geographical exactitude is not one of the ego's requirements; nor is factual correctness. If it could be established beyond doubt that the physical environment is utterly haphazard and without meaning, and that we are not firmly placed in a setting of reason, order, and logic, but rather are hopelessly lost, and are surrounded by an enormous agglomeration of senseless energy—still it would make no difference. The ego asserts anew that it is at the center, in the limelight, even though it does nothing but focus on itself.

A pristine beach in the center of the wilderness.

July 8

The wages of optimism

Ours only

BOTH THE MAP and the air photo indicated that we would have no trouble navigating the narrow channel from Andrecyk Lake to an unnamed lake to the west. We peered at the photo through a magnifying glass, and could see no white water in the channel. The map showed that both Andrecyk Lake and the unnamed lake had altitudes of 1315 feet.

We started off with optimism, anticipating that at the worst we would have to wade the canoe through some shallow water. But there turned out to be an elevation difference of six to eight feet, which meant hours of extreme labor. In some places we were in a channel scarcely more than twice the width of the canoe, heaving with all our strength and jamming it forward over the rocks a few feet or even only inches at a time. The heavily loaded canoe looked hopelessly incongruous in what was mainly a rock and forest setting. The last thirty feet of that snail-like portion of the trip required that we toss many rocks out of the channel, and to pry the larger ones out with a log, in order to make even a minimal passage for the canoe. Nevertheless we became hung up on the rocks, and had to throw two bags onto the bank to lighten the canoe so that we could wrench it on through. It beat portaging, however, which in that location would have been an all-day job, and a still more tiring one, since both banks of the channel were thickly overgrown. As it was it took us three hours to cover three-fourths of a mile.

We ate lunch on a high, rolling esker, and felt like the lords of all creation as we surveyed our unspoiled realm of dark blue water, white sand, and green spires of spruce. The sun was warm and there were few bugs, the most fortuitous combination imaginable.

We had two rugged portages in the afternoon across low, poorly drained land through "drunken forests"—incredible tangles of deadfalls and spindly trees tilting at precarious angles. The tilting was the result of heaving and sagging of the ground, brought about by fluctuations in the permafrost level.

We didn't stop until 8:00, moving slowly and not in the mood for much of anything but the mechanical task of setting up camp. Once again, though, psychological recuperation came quickly, brought about by rest, dry shoes and socks, and the prospect of a hot meal.

Aliens

Twilight was a soft orange and violet. About twenty degrees above the horizon, at such a distance that we could detect no sound, a vapor trail inched across the luminous sky. "There goes civilization," said John, and we left it at that. I felt only annoyance at such an intrusion, and the thought that crossed my mind was: "What! That insanity is still going on?" In our circumstances we found it impossible to consider men who were thousands of feet above the earth, ensconced in a winged tube of stainless steel and aluminum, traveling several hundred miles per hour, talking in flat, electronic voices—and on what errand? Surely we were not members of the same species.

July 9

WE HAD FISH for breakfast, and John, who in California said that he could never get enough fish, remarked that we were having fish too often and that he missed oatmeal. It was good to save on oatmeal, though, since we had only five and a half pounds left and it obviously wouldn't last the trip.

It was one of those days when I wanted to surrender completely to my natural affinity for idleness. We were camped in a good spot, and the weather was perfect for a day of minimal achievement. Would that we had had sufficient time and supplies so that on such a day we might say: "The hell with it! We like it here, and we don't feel like traveling today." And that would be that.

Banana Belt philosophy

We had brought with us all the worst habits of the Banana Belt. Too often we made the lamentable error of fixing our eyes and minds on the horizon, or on the distant goal of Snowdrift, or on one of the remote and nebulous objectives of civilized life. We would have been much the wiser, and perhaps more content as well, to focus the better part of our attention on all that was happening at our very feet. There was enough of interest within the reach of our senses to please us and keep us occupied throughout our lives. Sometimes I was bothered by the notion that in one important respect the trip was nothing more than a wilderness version of the economic rat race. We spent the best hours of our days in the compulsive performance of immoderate labors that exhausted our bodies and stifled our minds. And to what end? Why to the end, of course, that when the day's drudgery was done we would be free to sit back and enjoy life, if our faculties were not too dulled by then to experience enjoyment. Perhaps a practical man would have explained to us that all that work was necessary in order to go from here to there—without having the least notion of why it was desirable to go from one place to another, or without ever having entertained any doubt as to the desirability. We might best have explained our behavior by saying simply that we *wanted* to do it that way. But that was begging the question. No one could be certain why we were doing it—least of all ourselves.

Life's goals

We shoved off at the late hour of 11:30, paddled forty minutes, then had an easy portage of 300 yards. After a lunch of fish and the last of the raisin pie we felt like drowsing in the sun, but we overcame our slothful inclinations and set out again. We paddled an hour, portaged another 300 yards, paddled ten minutes in a channel through marshland, and made camp.

We were hopping from one small lake to another in order to reach Coventry Lake and the headwaters of the Taltson River. Another stretch of marshland was coming up after a half-mile paddle down the lake, although it was difficult to tell exactly on an aerial photo taken from 20,000 feet. I always hoped for the best and expected the worst. John, however, was the incurable optimist. He vigorously asserted that the forthcoming day's travel would present few obstacles and would be accomplished with a minimum of strain. Thus, before the fact, he decided that we should be able to go a certain distance; and then we knocked ourselves out trying to reach this arbitrarily established goal. We had constant friction on that point, and were unable to resolve it.

And how to attain them

July 10

JOHN SHOT A DUCK first thing in the morning. At the end of the lake was an impassable stream. It was only five or six feet wide, filled with huge boulders and littered with fallen trees. But at least the water was flowing our way. We were at the headwaters of the Taltson River, and it would be all downhill for more than 150 miles.

On the right bank at the head of the stream were some old axe cuttings and the remains of a prepared landing spot—the first human signs of any sort we'd seen since leaving Smalltree Lake. A third of a mile of good walking put us at the next lake, and we were afloat again. We paddled a mile and stopped for lunch: bannock, jam, and fish. John bagged another duck, so we gathered almost as much food as we consumed. We continued west with a fine tail wind, feeling cheerful about the prospects for an easy paddle through a marshy area which, on the photo, appeared to provide a good channel through to Gozdz Lake. The marshy area began well enough, but the sight of a large beaver lodge made us apprehensive. The channel soon split in two, then three, and

Home of the Northern Corps of Engineers.

within 200 feet there were dozens of channels tending off in all directions. We attempted to follow the current, but that proved as deceptive as both the size and direction of whatever channel we hoped was the main one. We soon found every channel blocked by a beaver dam, and the current dissipating through tall grass. We dragged the canoe over several dams, thinking that eventually we would break through to open water. But the channel we picked—and all others, as well as we could ascertain—gradually dwindled away to nothing. It became drier and more debris-filled until its dead-end in a swamp completely overgrown with tough, wiry bushes six feet high. What had once been the main stream was off to our right, blocked by an immense beaver dam, bone dry, and revealing a boulder-strewn bed. We unloaded onto a small patch of mud and brush, and portaged 250 feet over "ground" that was more liquid than solid, by far the worst portaging conditions we had ever experienced. Half the distance was through the tough wiry bushes. We plunged into them, stepping blindly and relying on the bushes for support even as they held us back. The remaining half was in knee-high marsh grass. Four trips apiece through that treacherous footing and sucking mud left us staggering and near collapse; we carried the canoe together, since it would have been folly for one man to try it alone. We were still in the marsh, but back into a fifteen-foot channel and only 200 yards from the lake. The "shore" was practically level with the water and floated the canoe almost as well. We loaded the canoe as it sat on the grass, and then shoved it in with ease. When we got to within thirty feet of the lake we found the entire area fenced in by the grandfather of beaver dams. There was the open water just beyond the dam, so near yet unattainable without more exhausting effort. With great fervor we cursed all beaver—past, present, and unto the furthest generation. That ritual out of the way, we dragged the bow onto the dam, unloaded, carried everything across, reloaded, and paddled out onto Gozdz Lake, slowly and without zest.

Dammed

The only good beaver is a . . .

We traveled another three miles and camped at eight o'clock on a fine sandy point. It was too good and obvious a spot to have been overlooked; there were signs of a very old Indian camp and a more recent survey camp. After changing into dry clothing we got to work on the food. We ate both ducks, mutually rejecting the notion of saving one for the next day's lunch. No need anyway. While the ducks were baking, John snagged two young jackfish in as many minutes. It was a fisherman's paradise, with the fish rushing in close to shore and contesting for the privilege of grabbing the hook. A large jackfish actually chased a smaller fish right up onto the sand. The jackfish swerved away at the last instant, but the small one had built up such momentum that he beached himself. He lay there for an instant, then with frantic flopping got back into the water again.

It was a nice site and a lovely calm evening. The view along the lake to the west was a mirror image of the view to the east; it looked as though half of it was real and the other half a reflection. But much of my capacity for enjoyment was lost in weariness; it had been the toughest day yet. If I had thought that the next day would offer only heavy toil to the point of exhaustion, I don't believe I would have got up in the morning. Better to die quietly in one's sleeping bag than to succumb to swamps and beaver dams.

Genteel departure

July 11

THE WORLD LOOKED BRIGHTER after a good sleep. We arose at 9:00, ate a leisurely breakfast of fried jackfish, and were on our way at noon. We paddled due west into a stiff wind; it took nearly two hours to cover four miles. After a lunch of fish and cold beans, we started down a three-mile-long channel leading to Coventry Lake and the Taltson River.

We had easy going for half a mile through grassland, then several hundred feet of wading through shallow water to the head of a turbulent rapids. As we came up to it, it looked extremely steep; the water disappeared as though on a slide or escalator. John spent twenty minutes surveying it, announced that we were going to run it, and we took off. It was a great pleasure to be traveling at such a clip. I was so exhilarated by the speedy ride that I had no sense of danger. There were curling waves two and three feet high in the center of the rapids. We bounded over and through them as rocks and trees flickered past on either side. Ten to fifteen gallons of water poured in over the bow, but we were through the rapids quickly and sped out into a small pond, throwing up a huge bow wave as we went.

From the air photo, we had picked out a good beach on Coventry Lake for a campsite, but we had quite a struggle getting there through heavy waves and a strong west wind we had been bucking all day. We charged ashore at eight o'clock with the waves and wind behind us. It was the best campsite yet. It faced west, overlooking a hundred-foot-wide beach. Back of the beach, and protected from the wind by a four-foot embankment, was a flat, smooth area for our tent and fire. We were plenty tired, and decided to spend a day there, resting up and repairing our clothing.

An esker, remnant of an Ice Age river, lying across the land like a gigantic bas-relief.

Windbound and White Water

July 12

THE MORNING was bright and clear. There was a blue sky overhead, but clouds were coming up from the southwest on a strong wind. We could see many whitecaps, and we probably couldn't have traveled if we had wanted to, since our course was due west across several miles of open water. After breakfast I repaired the soap dish with masking tape, the silverware bag with cellophane tape, and my underwear and pants with Jiffy Sew. John oiled his rifles, which were wet when we shipped water running the rapids. Both of us had sore backs, and the day of rest was much needed.

The wind and waves continued unabated, and by late afternoon the wind had blown up dark clouds. We stashed things away, covered them all with the tarps, and prepared for a big blow. But there was only a sprinkle, so John began making rice pudding. There was much mixing and cooking of various precious ingredients, followed by baking in the homemade oven. It turned out perfectly—half for dessert and half for the next day's lunch.

Rice pudding?

Except for an occasional dampening and a few prosaic chores, the day was ideal, the model on which we would wish most of our days to be patterned. That sort of life seemed to be more in harmony with our basic natures than anything else we know. At heart we were predatory roamers, as were our ancestors of many millennia ago. We were no more predatory than was necessary to keep our bellies full, but

Or predatory?

were always ready to wander—to see what was around the next bend and over the next hill.

There are desirable features of our lives on the Outside that we wouldn't relinquish, but when looked at from that remote position, most of the inventions and social arrangements of our society appear to be complications that confuse and stunt our lives.

Anyone who has had even a taste of the wilderness must at times succumb to the longing for a simpler existence. Somewhere, buried beneath the dross of civilized life, burns a secret spark of joy, a fond hope that the world can be made clean and pure again. Many men have gone to the North, but only a few have had the courage, or have been moved by the force of their dreams, to strive for salvation in a unity with nature. One of the few was John Hornby, an Englishman, who spent more than twenty years wandering the uninhabited reaches of the North. In a region where physical endurance is a common attribute, Hornby is remembered as one of the toughest of men—and perhaps most foolhardy as well. Often he went into the bush alone, taking with him only minimal equipment, neither expecting nor wanting anything the territory itself could not provide.

The graves of Edgar Christian, John Hornby, and Harold Adlard, a few feet from their cabin on the Thelon River.

In the fall of 1926 Hornby took his eighteen-year-old nephew, Edgar Christian, and another young man to spend the winter with him on the Thelon River, some 150 miles northeast of where John and I were. They had several rifles and much ammunition, intending to shoot enough caribou during the southward migration in the autumn to last them until spring. But the caribou did not come that year. The three men shot a few birds, trapped a few animals, suffered through the cold, dark winter, and slowly starved. Hornby died first, in April 1927. Adlard died in May, and Christian died in early June, just as life was returning to the North.

No caribou

Those who know of Hornby and his exploits talk about him with a strange ambivalence, a mixture of envy, fear, admiration, and resentment. Some say that he was the best of men but that he carried things to extremes, while others condemn him as a madman. Yet I think it is Hornby who, in their hearts, they all long to be.

It was now one month to the day since we had seen our last "others," the Indians camped at the beginning of the Chipman portage.

No others

July 13

RAIN BEGAN shortly after midnight and continued through dawn and well into the morning—a moderate but steady fall. A solidly overcast sky met our none-too-hopeful gaze as we peered out of the tent when we awoke. It was quite frustrating to be forced to lie flat, trying to get a few more minutes of unneeded sleep in this position or that, completely at the mercy of the weather.

Under conditions of enforced idleness my mind churned away on irrelevant, disconnected topics: the headline in the morning paper; the first-place team in the American League; the rush-hour traffic on the Los Angeles freeways—a real horror, that one! Though they were waking thoughts and images, they seemed like fragments of absurd dreams, wispy impressions from a previous incarnation. I could still convince myself that all that hectic activity went on as before, but my concern was waning and I no longer found it either funny or sad. It was just there, and it didn't mean very much. If that was the sort of life people on the Outside wanted, then let them have it—and the devil take them all.

No traffic

The rain soon stopped, so we dressed and eagerly sallied forth to our oatmeal. We had prudently stashed a few logs and some brush under the edge of the fly, and we had no trouble starting a fire. After eating, we lay on our raincoats by the fire and batted the breeze about a multitude of things. John is one of the few people I know who has remembered much of what he was taught, has correlated it with personal experience, and has made some sense out of it. Most people, upon finding that the reality of their lives bears little relation to what their education and upbringing led them to expect, will react in one of three ways: they develop the capacity to believe in mutually exclusive concepts at the same time; or they plump for one concept to the exclusion of all others; or, in some mysterious fashion, they allow experience and formal education to cancel each other, leaving the individual concerned in possession of a great bland nothing. The latter shouldn't be considered a total loss, however. As the words of the song have it: "Nothing from nothing is honest and square."

The mystery of life

In the evening we had a lengthy discussion of our favorite topic. I checked the Dri Lite supply and decided that we had enough to make it all the way, but there wouldn't be a large surplus as I initially had thought. Food was an obsession with both of us, although it was difficult to say why. We had an abundant supply, ate well every day, and had no worries beyond that of somewhat monotonous fare. However, our appetites were at least twice what they were back in the Banana Belt. About once a week we succumbed to our cravings, and ate double portions of whatever main course we were having.

Enamored

Food, frequently a nuisance or a time-consuming bore in the course of normal living, had become our first love. The absence of the many distractions of civilized life gave us plenty of time to contemplate nourishment, to discuss dishes once had and those we planned to have, to rhapsodize about a simple yet exotic luncheon of meat, cheese, bread, and wine. We became rapturous and ecstatic. What heavenly dreams and torments all this brought us! But we couldn't leave the subject alone—and this after less than five weeks with six or more still to go. We might well be at knife point across a few grains of rice before the trip was over.

There was no time of silence in the bush. Always there were bird calls or a rush of wind or the sound of moving water. What I missed was music. A Mozart or Vivaldi concerto would perfectly have suited my mood and that place.

Baroque music was needed—something calm, ordered, and logical to balance the chaos of nature.

John studying a map and thinking about what lies around a bend in the river or over the next hill.

July 14

WE WERE WINDBOUND. A string wind roared out of the southwest during the early hours of the morning, and by the time we arose it was tossing up large waves with many frothy whitecaps. From inside the tent it sounded like ocean surf. The wind abated during late afternoon, so we ate an early dinner and hoped to make eight or ten miles in the evening if the lake calmed.

During the day we discussed various ways of making enough money so as to be able to live entirely off the income from investments, leaving ourselves free to lead what we considered to be sane and intelligent lives. The alternative was dismal: work for its own sake is so futile and so dreadfully circumscribing. In the maxim of Oscar Wilde, "The sure way to know nothing about life is to try to make oneself useful." How could we amass enough money in a short time to be released from the necessity of leading a nose-to-the-grindstone existence, without being caught up in the insane game of acquiring money and property for their own sakes? How much is enough? How do we get to that point? How do we stop once we're there? We came to no conclusions, although we hashed over a number of possibilities—most of them of the get-rich-quick sort. The common idea of the road to financial success in the United States is: get up early in the morning, work hard, save your money . . . and strike oil. Actually there are many legitimate and plausible ways to make money in the United States, but the paradox is that freedom from those activities was precisely what we sought. The entire concept of plunging into the money-making whirl struck us as petty, degrading, and—above all—incredibly stupefying. Well, enough said about money for the rest of the trip. Our cash and traveler's checks were hidden away, and would not be brought to light until we reached Snowdrift and needed some means of contending with the Outside.

Getting free

Getting well

The wind and waves picked up again, and we were unable to travel in the evening. We were not in a hurry—merely impatient. The daily routine, the aesthetic pleasures, and the stimulating conversation continued as usual, but our lives had lost their meaning if we were not propelling ourselves through the wilderness by canoe or—heaven forbid!—on foot. Motion, the simple act of going forward into new territory with Snowdrift as the ultimate goal, was the quintessence of our lives.

July 15

ANOTHER COLD NIGHT. Both of us slept poorly, and we were doing our best sleeping as the sun rose at the start of a beautiful day. Our course was west for seven miles, and then we turned north into the beginning of the Taltson River and paddled another three miles to the first rapids, a narrow spot where the river cut through an esker. The rapids dropped only a foot. It was deep water with a hundred feet of swift current, and we sped through it with no trouble.

Going down the Taltson

On we went down the river, which was as much as half a mile wide in places. The sun was warm enough to permit removing our shirts. At 5:00 we came to the second rapids. The river, which had been flowing north, abruptly turned west into a channel 150 feet wide. The first half of the rapids could safely be run, but the next portion was too hazardous and there was no intervening section of calm water where we could reduce speed and get to shore. We waded the canoe down over large and slippery rocks, getting wet to the waist in the process.

It was slow, painstaking work, but it beat portaging and we couldn't afford to risk running a rapids where the chances of getting through were less than fifty-fifty. There was no one around to fish us out should we overturn, no way to replenish lost food or equipment, and no way to replace a smashed canoe. The trip thus far had been without danger, and neither of us had been ill or injured. We were now so accustomed to that style of life and found our surroundings so familiar and harmonious that we sometimes tended toward complacency. Recalling that we had to depend entirely on ourselves, and reminding each other of the hazards we faced, served to keep us on our toes and to reassure us that we were taking the proper precautions.

John hooked a jackfish in the pool at the foot of the rapids. It was 7:30 when we landed, and by the time we had dinner and washed the dishes it was after 11:00—much too late and much too long a day. We made the same old tired resolution about improving our schedule, but we didn't turn in until 12:30.

We did about eighteen miles. Very good.

July 16

SHORTLY BEFORE NOON we came to the head of a major rapids. It posed the same problem as the previous one. Much of it could be run, but halfway down was a turbulent stretch that was a tossup—the fifty-fifty proposition again. There was no way to avoid it once we started the easily-run stretch above; we would be committed.

Lining, wading, paddling

We lined the canoe down along the right bank. John guided the bow with a long pole, and I kept the canoe close to shore and regulated the speed with a line attached to the stern. We made good time, hopping from boulder to boulder and not even getting our feet wet. Unfortunately, following the right bank eventually put us in slack current and shallow water. We got hung up on the rocks several times, were in the water up to our knees, and had to heave and shove to bull our way through. It took us a solid two hours to negotiate the entire rapids—about a third of a mile and a drop of sixteen feet. We dawdled after lunch, drying our socks and boots in the sun. With the previous day's long traveling and the effort

The most aggravating chore was the daily unpacking and repacking.

of getting down the rapids, we were somewhat lacking in energy and ambition. We paddled on slowly for about an hour, and turned east into the channel leading to Dymond Lake. At once we were running into a strong headwind, and fighting waves that were as large as we cared to be in. Our fatigue and the futility in crawling along against the wind took us to the north bank to make camp at 4:45.

Futility

We discussed our mutual lassitude. It was undoubtedly due in part to the physical demands we made of ourselves on some days, and to the emotional stress placed on us by certain activities such as running rapids or wading the canoe down them. John theorized that dietary deficiencies might be partly to blame; he thought that Dri Lite foods might have lost vital elements in the dehydration process. We needed more meat, he believed, although we had been eating lots of fish and fowl and should have been getting enough protein. We agreed that boredom was at times a contributing factor. Most of the time we were engaged in traveling, or were occupied with various tasks around camp. But that was too dull a routine for two of the products of a swift-paced, diverting, complex society. Now and again we were afflicted with ennui, and wished there were something to amuse us or occupy our minds. It was the common contemporary malaise: sitting and waiting, and wondering "why doesn't something happen?"

Boredom

Luckily neither of us was bored or dissatisfied with the other's company, nor were we consciously aware of having had but a sole human contact for five weeks. We had had minor disagreements, some of them quite aggravating to both of us, but we both had sense enough to realize that it was absolutely necessary to get along together, and we always pulled in our horns before a difference of opinion or argument got out of hand. John had many habits and idiosyncracies that rubbed me the wrong way, but he wasn't the sort of person whom one reforms, so I ignored those annoyances as best I could. Undoubtedly I had habits that

Getting along

grated on him. But his good qualities far outweighed his minor shortcomings. In most respects John was exactly the sort of companion one wanted on a journey such as ours. He was strong, resourceful, able to tolerate the hardships and perform the extreme labor required, and definitely not the type to collapse psychologically when the going got rough. Furthermore, we were intellectually compatible to a considerable degree, which to my mind was one of the more important requirements. I wouldn't have been able to put up with a dunderhead for that length of time.

July 17

PERSEVERANCE AND SELF-INDOCTRINATION paid off, and we finally made an early start. We spent a tough morning paddling east through the remainder of the channel and then north on Dymond Lake to where the Taltson began again. There was a strong wind, generally from the east but channeled by various islands; it seemed that no matter what direction we went we had a headwind. And the waves were bad; frequently they came from two directions at once, making handling of the canoe tricky and causing us to ship some water. We had a lunch of cold beans and chocolate bars about a mile above the first of three rapids in a two-mile stretch of river.

Our routine at a rapids was for John, the stern man, to scout ahead and decide how we would take it—by running it, wading, or a portage. We pulled into the bank as close to the head of the rapids as possible without letting the current get us, John went ashore and walked downstream to see how it looked, while I sat and waited, daydreaming or writing my journal.

The first two rapids posed no problem, and we ran them with ease. The third rapids was approximately 120 yards long. It was deep, swift, and very turbulent with three-foot-high curling waves in the center. John scouted it carefully and decided that it was safe to run, but it turned out to be more violent than it had appeared from the bank. The waves seemed to tower over us, and I had the sensation that we were charging into a deep rift in the river whose steep sides of water threatened to collapse into the canoe at any moment. Within thirty yards we began shipping water over the bow, and by the time we reached the halfway point we were taking in huge

amounts. Each wave that gushed in made us lower in the water and more vulnerable to the next one, a cumulative process that quickly overwhelmed us. It happened so fast that there was no time to become frightened. My only emotion was incredulity. It simply didn't seem possible that our canoe, the major stable object in our lives, was about to founder. Then for an instant I had the thought that we must appear inept and ludicrous, and I was glad there was no one on shore watching us; it simply wouldn't do to become the laughingstock of the forest. When we reached the foot of the rapids we were swamped. The canoe was full of water, and all that kept us from going to the bottom were the flotation compartments in the bow and stern, and our two boxes, which were afloat and pulling upward on the ropes tying them into the canoe. The fine job John did in holding the canoe straight saved us from possible disaster. Had we turned sideways in such rough water we would have capsized and might have lost part of our outfit.

Swamped

At the foot of the rapids we swerved left into a calm pool and wallowed through the water toward shore like a submerged garbage scow fighting a fast current. We looked ridiculous, I'm sure. We were sitting in water to our waists, with the top third of our baggage poking above the water between us—and the canoe was completely out of sight. The absurdity of the sight struck me, and loudly I sang "Row, row, row your boat, gently down the stream." It got a laugh out of John, and improved my mood, too—just what we needed.

Submarining

There wasn't a good landing spot, and we were unable to get all the way to shore. We unloaded everything onto a jumble of boulders while standing in water to our knees, dumped the water from the canoe, then reloaded and headed downstream again. Only half an hour elapsed from the start of our run down the rapids to the time we were reloaded after the mishap and on our way again. We continued another mile and a half until we found a strip of gravel beach, with an acceptable spot for our tent back among the trees.

As soon as we landed we spread the tarps and unpacked every single piece of our gear. We were quite apprehensive about what we might have lost to water damage, especially flour, tea, oatmeal, and other perishables. Much to our relief we found that we had lost nothing; the precaution of having everything tied into waterproof bags paid off. Then too, the Woods bags and our sturdy boxes came close to keeping out all water for the short time they were immersed—not more than ten minutes, and never deep enough for water to get in the top of them. Both of us were surprised that we were not as dismayed as we thought we should be by such a near catastrophe. If we had lost our canoe or crucial parts of our outfit, we might well have had trouble ever getting out of there. But we not only came out smelling like a rose, we actually benefited from the swamping. In the course of checking over every food item for damage, I discovered, deep in the bag containing the reserve oatmeal supply, our long-lost, lamented yeast. It was in fine shape, safely wrapped in its own waterproof bag. The next time we stopped for a day or two John would bake bread. The drying and partial repacking of the gear took until midnight, but we didn't mind the work since we considered ourselves fortunate to have gotten off scot-free.

Serendipity

July 18

IN THE MORNING we ran a 200-yard-long rapids, plowing through a few feet of curling waves and shipping about an inch of water—just enough to make it interesting. Then downstream to the next rapids, quite a long one making a sweeping S-curve. The upper and lower parts were okay, but in the middle was a turbulent stretch worse than the one that almost did us in. It wasn't practical to break it up into segments, so we portaged half a mile over generally good footing in open terrain. It was our first portage in eight days.

We camped on an attractive sand plain. It was mostly open ground with tall scattered trees, sitting on a rise ten feet above the water. There were signs of an old camp. It had been made by white men, judging by a stack of neatly cut logs. The Indians never bother to chop logs in the white man's fashion. They simply put several trees in the fire, and as the ends are consumed they push the trees farther in.

Predecessors

During the afternoon we talked about what seems to be the permissiveness of American society. It is generally accepted in the United States that a person should be, and is, allowed to do and say as he pleases, within loose and flexible bounds; and that this is because the United States is a democracy, an open society. But the political, economic, and social structures of any given country are of no moment: capitalist and socialist countries are afflicted by the same maladies, varying only in the degree to which they have perfected the techniques of industrial organization and control. Ennui, rage, self-hatred, and self-contempt are the common heritage of East and West, engendered by the subconscious knowledge that the quality of our lives and the thrust of our societies are dictated to us by our own inventions. Will we refuse the application of new machines once they have come into being? No, of course we will not. Invariably we succumb to the technological imperative, the irresistible demand that when a machine has been created it

Author keeping an eye on dinner. Collecting firewood usually required no more effort than bending over to pick it up.

must be used, when something becomes possible it *will* be done—if for no other reason than that the creators of new devices cannot bear to see their children rust or rot.

The ethos of the machine is Order and Efficiency. Though these are not *human* concerns they now transcend all else. We are intrigued and mesmerized by them, have embraced them warmly, and are making every effort to adapt ourselves to them. Men are haunted by their dreams, and if mankind could dream collectively it might well dream only of Order and Efficiency—at any price. The machine cannot dream, want, hate, love, but it is itself dreamed of, wanted, hated, loved. We have cast our lot with the machine. With an insane, ecstatic joy—and never a backward look—we have relegated feet to better tires, brains to swifter computers, fists to missiles.

First love

We call these changes triumph, but it is defeat on a grand scale. The technological system is inexorable. It is rolling down a grade, gaining momentum, gathering more souls, snowballing into the future, a future that bids fair to be a machine-ridden purgatory, a new paradise lost where it will be small consolation to say, "Better to reign in hell than serve in heaven."

Were John and I actively to oppose the extension of technical organization to all realms of life we would become enemies of the people, or, more correctly, enemies of the State. But not to oppose it is to become enemies of ourselves—yet to no avail. It is a wretched choice.

The only valid choice remaining is withdrawal to the position of observer, student, witness. It is, perhaps, a position that many more people would be striving for had they given more consideration to a choice of occupation. But for most, the opportunity to choose is never there; or else they are strangers to the idea that one should even endeavor to choose. Too quickly they are caught up in the rush and whirl of modern life, and their only thought is to clutch at the first chip or straw to come drifting by, whether or not it is what they wished to embrace, so that they will not be overwhelmed altogether.

Last chance

We were treated to a magenta-orange sunset. The glow made it feel like a warmer night than it actually was. John asked if I would stay up there alone all winter if someone provided me with a cabin and 3,000 pounds of supplies of my own choosing.

Certainly! But who's going to do that, John?

A Shaky Grip on Life

July 19

WE WERE UP at 7:00 again. It was good to know that we could do it if we wanted to. But we weren't carried away by pride at our modest accomplishment. Routine has been the ruin of many a good man, and if we didn't watch our step we might find ourselves commuting to work and joining clubs that meet regularly.

There was blue sky to the northwest, but low gray clouds directly overhead and blacker ones coming up from the southeast. We bolted our orange juice, oatmeal, and tea, and cooked up a batch of chili for lunch—the only item on the menu for noon. At 9:15 we were on the water, and ran two mild rapids during the first hour. Later the river turned west and widened out to half a mile. We had a tail wind and made wonderful time—fourteen miles behind us when we stopped for lunch at the head of the next rapids.

After we ate, John caught a thirty-four-inch jackfish and shot a duck. With the food situation looking up but the weather darkly threatening again, we ran a rapids that was about 400 feet long and had a considerable number of two-foot waves in it. We shipped increasingly large amounts of water as we went, and at one point we were virtually out of control, broadside to the current with both of us paddling for all we were worth in an effort to get straightened away. We had five inches of water sloshing around in the canoe as we headed into the last twenty yards of the rapids. It made us ride so low that with a sharp jolt we ran aground on some rocks. In an instant we leaped out, freed the canoe, and waded it through water up to our thighs to a calm spot. We

Water water everywhere

reboarded and paddled to shore, where we quickly unloaded, dumped the water, reloaded, and at once ran another one hundred feet of frothy rapids. All of this happened so fast that we had no time to become worried or fearful; there was never a chance to take a long cool look at our situation—which was just as well. That was the second time in three days we had almost come to grief.

Out on the broad river again we made good speed with a strong tail wind, and increasingly heavy waves rolling up on us from astern. We had intended to paddle another two hours, soaked or not, but the waves made us reconsider. We pulled to shore and camped on a sand plain. John shot another duck, a full-grown one with three times the meat on it as the duckling he had bagged earlier.

We camped on a sand plain. Just a few miles farther north, most of the country was treeless.

There was a monotonous procession of light and dark clouds, spates of rain, and small patches of blue sky parading past from the east as though on a production line. We chopped down five small trees, cut off their branches, and rigged up one of the tarps for a lean-to. We sat under the lean-to with rain pattering on the roof. The fish and two ducks were wrapped in aluminum foil and buried under the fire, and corn and macaroni were heating on the grill above it.

A herd of low clouds was rushing westward down the river. All the weather in that part of the world moves at a rapid pace. The wind was blowing strongly from the east, from Hudson Bay, notorious for its inclement weather. The trip was approximately half over in terms of time, and a bit more than halfway in distance. If we could make it up to Eileen Lake by August 1, we would be able to take four or five days off and do some good relaxing.

July 20

WE DID PLENTY OF RELAXING, but not because we'd planned it. The rain continued all through the night and into the morning. There was a three-hundred-foot ceiling, with dripping clouds still rushing downstream. It was a sodden, dull day, dampening our spirits as well as everything else. John started a fire with chunks of rotten wood from the interior of a log, and we gathered fuel enough to last the day.

John made the first reference to food early in the morning. He suggested that when we get back to Edmonton we treat ourselves to one top-notch meal: steak with all the trimmings, preceded by drinks and followed by whatever the occasion demands. I heartily agreed, having had the same thought for the past couple of weeks.

The bakery

About 8:00 in the evening, undaunted by the continuing foul weather and finding it impossible to restrain himself, John decided to bake two loaves of bread—our refound yeast getting its first workout. He mixed the dough and rigged up his oven despite the rain; he seemed to delight in coping with the most adverse conditions. The first half hour of baking was done with the oven too close to the fire, so that a fine crust developed but the interiors and bottoms of the loaves were underdone. John solved the problem by turning the loaves upside down in the pans and giving them another twenty minutes. They turned out well, and we would have bread for a week if we ate it sparingly.

Serious dialogue

We talked about nothing but food all day. How idiotic! It seemed that we were gradually evolving a food-centered culture—which, when I thought about it, was not idiotic but perfectly rational. Food was life and balm and solace, and a substitute for our accustomed pursuits and diversions. It was only fitting that we should accord it the number one spot in our hierarchy of values.

Although the primitive life gave us a kind and degree of freedom that is not to be had in civilization, we had paid a price for it. We were captives of the environment, and of the state of mind engendered by that captivity. Yet there is something far worse. Men have built vast, complex civilizations and thereby escaped from a total dependency on nature, but in spite of enormous expenditures and immense efforts have succeeded merely in exchanging one form of captivity for another. And perhaps lost ground in the bargain, for now we are prisoners of ourselves and of the artificial environment we have created. It may be that we are the victims and not the beneficiaries of everything we have done. This is a burden as heavy as—and perhaps even more humiliating than—being subject to a natural environment over which we have no control.

A bad bargain

July 21

WE SPENT THE MORNING conversing, and positioning our boots and clothing to gain maximum drying effect from the fire. John remarked that to make such a journey a complete experience we should have had women along—wives, mistresses, or husky concubines. I agreed that it would be fine to have women to share our sleeping bags at night, but where were we going to find women willing to undertake such a journey? The days of tough squaws are long gone.

A matter of taste

But perhaps we wouldn't even want tender squaws. Samuel Hearne wrote: "Ask a Northern Indian, what is beauty? he will answer, a broad flat face, small eyes, high cheekbones, three or four broad black lines across each cheek, a low forehead, a large broad chin, and breasts hanging down to the belt."

This line of thought led to a discussion of sex, which topic we disposed of in a couple of minutes. We simply weren't interested. We had no desire, didn't feel in the least deprived, and seldom even thought about women. But it wasn't surprising. We saw no women, and there were none of the stimulants of civilization: shouting billboards, suggestive advertisements and commercials, verbal allusions, erotic forms of dress, and all the other references and reminders that beat upon one's senses every hour of the day. Furthermore, we were preoccupied with the details of the trip; our days were filled with tasks that consumed all our thought and energy. When we were not engrossed in whatever we were doing, we were usually so weary and hungry that we thought only of rest and food. Briefly we hashed over the idea of marriage, but we couldn't think of a way to reconcile marriage with that style of life. Yes, a couple of minutes sufficed, and then our thoughts turned to maps, logistics, the fire, weather, and food. After all, what else is there?

Looking across the Taltson River.

July 22

ANOTHER OVERCAST DAY, the fourth in succession. Rows of gray clouds proceeded stolidly westward driven by a damp breeze. When we started across McArthur Lake it seemed calm enough to be navigated, but it caught us with our guard down when we reached the open water exposed to the wind. There were no whitecaps to indicate what we were getting into, and by the time we were on the open lake it was too late to turn back. Immense swells came rolling up from astern and threatened to engulf us. They were headed in our direction, but the proper course was the least of our worries. We doubled the normal rate of paddling to maintain enough headway for John to control the canoe. As the larger swells passed beneath us, first the stern and then the bow were lifted completely out of the water. When the stern was out there was an unnerving roller-coaster and fishtailing effect. Several times John shouted, "Paddle harder!" If I had had any wind I would have replied that I was almost pulling my arms out of their sockets with every stroke. As the swells surged past my bow position I winced and held my breath; I was certain water would come pouring in at any moment. But we shipped not a drop, being just buoyant enough to keep the bow and gunwales from going under. If we had had one inch less freeboard we would have taken on water from the larger swells, and quickly been swamped. And to be swamped in the middle of the lake, two miles from shore, might have finished off our gear—and us.

In peril

We drove toward the gray-green shore with its line of low trees, a strip of beach, and flecks of white where waves were breaking on boulders at the water's edge. It took twenty minutes at fifty strokes to the minute, an all-out effort that barely pulled us through. Finally we rounded a point and left the lake for the continuation of the Taltson River. I was perspiring freely in spite of the cool air, and my arms felt as though I would never be able to use them again. While it was happening we were too busy paddling to think about the worst possible consequences. Even when it was all over we couldn't find the words to express our fears, and had to fall back on such phrases as "that was pretty rough," and "it had me worried there for a while."

Six miles down the Taltson we came to two rapids. We ran the first one, but the second was fairly turbulent. Our earlier experiences with rough rapids had made us cautious, and the crossing of McArthur Lake had brought to mind the desirability of living to a ripe old age. We waded the canoe down in forty minutes, getting wet to just above the knees—our daily one-third bath. We put in at once on a good beach and campsite in a cove.

Longevity looks good

It rained off and on during the evening, the wind was from the east, and there was a solid overcast. John fell asleep while reading by the fire. We had made eighteen to twenty miles.

July 23

THE DAY BEGAN with an overcast and the threat of rain. Some of the simple and previously unnoticed things had become central features of our lives, and very gratifying they were: the warmth of a fire; the thought of dry clothes when we were wading rapids; and, the ultimate desire when I was cold and tired, a euphoric anticipation of how nice it would be when I was all decked out in my thermal underwear and warmly ensconced in my sleeping bag. Nothing could ever be better! Too bad we would no longer enjoy those minor aspects of life to such a degree when we returned to the Outside. Once again our lives would be filled with diversions, entertainments, and potential satisfactions, but we would be less easily satisfied, and seldom content.

John, the optimist, apparently believed in the perfectibility of man. Although man is now irrational at times, all he needs to achieve rationality is education. John's thesis was that the proper level of education might be attained in a generation or two in the United States and other countries that can produce sufficient goods to provide the average man with material comfort. Then, John thought, men would be happy with what they had and would devote their efforts to becoming wise and rational. John professed to see a definite trend in that direction, while my view was quite the opposite. The more a man gets the more he wants, and the more he strives for what he wants the fewer are those moments of respite when he may think upon the world and life. And as for irrationality, it is not to be educated away or overcome in any other manner. The irrational is part of us; it's in the bloodstream.

Author wading the canoe down the Taltson—the daily one-third bath.

We traveled four hours in the afternoon. It was a short day, but half that time was spent in wading down a long and violent rapids—an annoying, laborious task. When we started down the rapids, a south wind was quickly blowing away the clouds. We had an hour of sunshine. How wonderful it felt after five days of overcast! But by the time we made camp, the wind switched to the north and blew a black cloud bank across the sun. We had covered about five miles. At that rate we might arrive at Snowdrift on ice skates rather than by canoe.

Snail's pace

I confessed to having been quite upset by the dangerous crossing of McArthur Lake, but the only change induced by that frightening twenty minutes was increased prudence. For John, however, the experience seemed to have been somewhat traumatic. Several times since then he mentioned what a close call it was, but to my embarrassment he seemed concerned more for me than for himself. He said that he felt responsible for my safety, since the idea for the trip was his and because he evidently felt that its successful completion depended on his wilderness skills—which I admit were much better developed than mine.

A gambler

But one's knowledge and skill were only half the game. John was a gambler, and at times was so intent on covering more miles that his headlong approach to life got us into dangerous situations. I was more cautious by nature, and though my experience was not so great as John's I was much less inclined to take chances. John felt challenged by obstacles and difficulties, and waxed optimistic to show that he was undaunted by the challenges. Then he acted on the basis of his unfounded optimism. People like that make dangerous, or even deadly, traveling companions.

An innocent

Although I suspect that John often regarded me as a babe in the woods, it was nice to know that *someone* was concerned for my welfare. With John and I both looking after me, surely I would come to no harm.

A Diet of Moose

July 24

WE HEADED DUE NORTH across a small lake, and in half an hour we came to the stream and rapids leading from the lake. We stopped on the right to scout it, but the water was too shallow and rocky to let us get all the way ashore. Also, the left seemed to be the better side from which to survey the rapids. We were in a calm pool about a hundred feet above the rapids, having already come down 150 feet of increasingly fast current, so we had to cross the current to reach the left side. This we did by heading upstream, paddling hard, and, at a very slight angle to the current, edging over the way we wished to go. We started out in good style, but the stern was suddenly caught by an unnoticed back current that spun us 270 degrees—and in an instant we were broadside in the middle of the stream and floating down upon the rapids. The force of the current heeled us over, and water poured into the canoe. We were over so far that John and I came near to being thrown out. We hung on, and managed to right the canoe—by then full of water—and with furious paddling made it back to the pond we had just left.

Learning process

Then followed the same exhausting process of unloading the canoe on bad footing in water, dumping water from the canoe, and reloading. We were getting pretty good at it—experience tells. That particular experience shook us up a good deal, and since we were thoroughly wet already we waded the canoe down the rapids. As we never tired of reminding each other, such incidents were potentially disastrous. Had we capsized and gone through the rapids in that state, we easily could have lost both the canoe and our gear, without

Morbid thoughts

which we were lost indeed. We could see ourselves—gaunt, emaciated, crawling on hands and knees in the general direction of Snowdrift, falling on our faces as the last bit of strength ebbed away, and in the sand scratching deathless last words—that were washed away by rain the following day. Time passed, and one became morbid. Perhaps it was all a joke, and the best thing to do was laugh. But we couldn't do it. We were lost on a lonely planet. Life was fragile and tenuous—and so precious.

We paddled across a small lake, became confused by some islands, and took a wrong turning. After half an hour of hard paddling against a headwind and waves we found ourselves in a cul-de-sac. Disgusted, we landed on a convenient sheltered beach and removed our shoes and pants for a spell of drying in brilliant warm sunshine. But just as we finished lunch a brief rain squall hit, and we were wet all over again.

Nature in control

In the afternoon we crossed a small lake, and wearily waded the canoe down a long, rough rapids. We started across a larger lake, and had made half a mile when a strong wind with huge waves came rushing at us. It was too much for us to buck, so we turned around and attempted to run back to a fine beach and campsite that was astern and slightly to the right of us—but we couldn't get there. The waves were so large that we couldn't angle across them to the slightest degree. They carried us back past the point we had rounded shortly before. We ducked into the lee of the point to wait for the wind and waves to moderate, and perched ourselves on a protruding boulder in shallow water fifty feet off shore.

After emptying our boots and wringing out our socks, we discussed the affairs of the world. It was a most incongruous scene: probably the only human beings within a radius of a hundred miles, perched like two soggy cats on a hunk of rock surrounded by water, waiting meekly for a change in the weather, and all the while hashing over the problems of the organized society from which we had temporarily escaped. Perhaps it was a good indication that permanent escape was not possible.

In half an hour conditions improved enough for us to sneak back around the point and reach the campsite. Two things had priority when we stopped at the end of the day: dry clothes, and a big fire. Gathering firewood usually was a cinch; there was dead, dry wood everywhere, and one needed only to pick it up. If use of the axe was necessary, properly dry logs three or four inches in diameter could be broken with one or two blows.

Just as we finished dinner and I was putting the kettle on the fire to heat for dishwashing, I glanced at the lake and saw a young cow moose standing in two feet of water about twenty yards from shore. She was regarding us with great curiosity.

John's .270 was lying on the poncho directly behind him. He grabbed it, aimed, fired—and the moose didn't move a muscle. The distance was less than a hundred yards, and we couldn't believe that it was a clean miss. Then she took several slow steps farther out into the lake, keeled over,

A killing

thrashed about for ten seconds, and was dead. We jumped into the canoe, paddled over to her, attached a rope around her neck, and with furious paddling succeeded in dragging her to a spot opposite our campsite. It wasn't possible to get her through the shallows that way, so we waded her in by hand to the beach. We estimated that she weighed 300 pounds; with a lot of heaving and grunting we hauled her up on the sand. We gloated over the kill and the prospect of a great feast.

Yet at the same time I felt regretful and a bit ashamed that we had killed the moose. We needed the food, but I would prefer to carry all my sustenance with me, leave the land unchanged, and kill nothing.

July 25

UP AT FIVE O'CLOCK, an unspeakable hour. The first business of the day was to slice off several large choice cuts of moose meat and a panful of liver, and have a hearty breakfast. The liver and steaks were delicious. We also sampled the tongue, the heart, the kidneys, and the brains; all of it hit the spot. There was much smacking of lips and exclaiming to

A feast

each other over the flavor, texture, and aroma—a great use of superlatives and expressions of unbounded joy.

Than the work began. John cut and trimmed the meat, slicing much of it into six-inch-long strips, which we attempted to smoke and dry. There was also the liver and twenty-five to thirty larger chunks of meat for taking with us. I chopped several trees for a lengthy fire. We rigged three parallel wires about a foot apart and twelve to fourteen inches above the ground. We were unable to make a good smoky fire, so we hung the strips of meat on the wires and used the heat and flames for a combination scorching and drying. We didn't know how effective that would be, especially because the deer flies were out in force and were trying to lay their eggs on our meat. There was no time to fix the meat in the Indian fashion—hanging the strips on a line or spreading them on boulders in the sun and letting them dry for several days to make jerky.

John sweating over a hot fire to dry and scorch strips of moose.

We dined on liver and steaks again at lunch, and spent the early afternoon sweating over a hot fire and being toasted by a warm sun. We finally got under way at 4:00. Halfway across the lake we were hit by a strong wind that built up large waves in a few minutes. We had to head directly into the wind, about ninety degrees off course. We didn't ship any water other than a few light splashes, but dozens of waves came within a fraction of an inch of pouring over the bow.

Perverse lake

Then a ferocious rain squall hit us. We didn't dare stop paddling to put on our rain gear, and we were soaked from head to toe. It was our first complete wetting since our stay on Smalltree Lake twenty days earlier. We made it safely to the lee of a small island where we changed into dry shirts. In half an hour the wind let up and we were able to get back on course and into the river again, relieved to be done with such a perverse lake. We did another two miles and made camp. For the evening meal we had, of course, moose steaks and liver, supplemented by modest portions of mashed potatoes and a vegetable. We gorged ourselves, but didn't feel stuffed even though we put away at least two pounds of meat apiece.

Good intentions

Earlier, when we were temporarily stranded on the small island, we decided that we simply *must* cover more miles. We had been so careless about our schedule that we had fallen behind. We would have to travel even on foul days if we hoped to catch up to our original timetable and get to Snowdrift by August 25. To cover more miles we would try to get up at 6:00, leave at 8:00, and not stop until 6:00 in the evening. But if we traveled too late then sack time came so late as to prohibit an early rising. What with a lengthy dinner and some chores to do, we didn't turn in until 11:30.

July 26

WE HAD A LARGE BREAKFAST of liver and steak, and departed at 10:30. We had not gone more than half a mile from our campsite when we were exposed to the wind. We continually had to tack this way and that, paddling two or three miles to gain one. An hour of that annoying activity saw us out of the lake and headed down the river. Literally down, for the river dropped more than a hundred feet in a stretch of twenty miles. The day consisted of painfully slow progress through a succession of rapids. There were five in all, separated by small placid ponds or short stretches of stream with little current. We ran two and waded three, and camped at the foot of the final one. The landing was on a smooth rock shelf much like a beach—an area of bedrock covered with a two-inch overlay of moss and lichens.

A lesson learned

The trip had taught us calmness, and developed in us a considerable degree of patient endurance. A good thing it was, else we could not have stood the contemplation of the minute distance we traveled on some of those days; it hardly seemed commensurate with the effort expended. It was true that we liked to see the miles go by, but we had learned not to attack nature with desperation. Sooner or later, if we kept plugging away, we would get to where we wished to go. Those who are imbued with the Banana Belt ethic, which requires one to travel to many places with the greatest possible speed, might be inclined to sneer at our creeping pace and to doubt that we would ever achieve any objective. I in turn would observe that none of those who travel on jet planes have yet reached any of the places that John and I visited on our journey, nor are they likely to.

Gracious living

We ate immense amounts of liver and steak for dinner. The meal was spread out over two hours of slow eating, conversation, and then frying up another panful. Although sated, we were now having food desires and fantasies of a different sort: how we missed our oatmeal for breakfast, how good it would have been to have bread and jam for lunch, how—after six straight meals of moose—we craved variety. We had full bellies and a full larder, yet food was still an obsession. We probably wouldn't get over those wishes and dreams until we had been on the Outside long enough to satisfy our special cravings (such as a lunch of French bread, bologna with hot mustard, a Gouda cheese, and a bottle of red wine), and were reassured that food of all sorts was close at hand. The first food store we hit in Edmonton was sure going to catch hell.

July 27

UP EARLY, but feeling strangely lethargic. We had a large, heavy breakfast of liver and steak. It was the last of the liver, which was beginning to get flabby and lose its shape. Both of us were very sluggish and slow. We were not even in the mood for talk, and passed most of the morning in silence.

In half a mile we came to a short rapids, which we ran. Then half a mile across a small lake, a serene and lovely spot with good beaches and studded with many look-alike islands. Next came a long and rough rapids, about 250 yards, which we waded slowly. We did everything slowly; normal tasks took on the dimensions of vast labors. Our impulse was to lie on the nearest level spot, and wait for unconsciousness to put us out of our misery.

Vast labors

Immediately after wading the rapids we stopped for an early lunch: dried moose, tea, and—wanting something sweet—half a dozen spoonfuls each of plum jam. Then we crossed another lake, twice the size of the previous one and of similar appearance. We came to a long and heavy rapids, one of the few that was marked on the map. It was too rough for wading, so we had to portage two-fifths of a mile. We moved at a crawl all afternoon, and didn't finish the portage until 5:30, being by that time utterly spiritless.

We crossed the river and made camp at once. It was an exhausting effort to unload the canoe and carry the tent and cooking gear a few feet up the slope. That experience, in my view, exploded John's theory that our occasional lapses of

Three hours of wading was preferable to a one-mile portage.

energy and alertness were due to a lack of fresh meat in our diet. I still thought they were largely psychological, especially when we knew that the forthcoming day would be tough. Both of us were heartily sick of the Taltson River with its never-ending rapids. We would be very glad to get off that river and on to something else, even though that future something might prove to be more difficult. During the evening we both felt a physical rejuvenation—for mental reasons, if my theory was correct.

July 28

WE PUT AWAY our customary three panfuls of moose steak, and shoved off. In half an hour we came to the longest rapids marked on the map. John took forty minutes to scout it, and returned to announce that there was a good mile of continuous rough water and that it looked like five to six hours of wading. My first view down the full length of the rapids appalled me, as it had John. The lake into which the river flowed, with a beautiful sand bluff on its far shore, seemed to be at an impossible distance. However, the wading turned out to be not too bad—better footing and fewer serious obstructions than we had encountered in previous rapids. The gradient was constant, which made for a steady flow of water and few deeps or shallows. But the task wore us down.

Walking in water

We stumbled and slipped over footing we could hardly see, and were constantly bent over to hang onto the canoe. We kept at it steadily, and made it to the bottom of the rapids in three hours flat. Then we stood erect once again, climbed into the canoe, and paddled to the west end of the lake to have a late lunch and dry our clothes on a sunny beach.

What wild oscillations! From hours of putting out extravagant amounts of energy to an interval of complete idleness. But no matter how great the expenditure of our physical resources, the eventual reward was more than adequate. We sprawled half naked on an unsullied beach, gnawing on strips of dried moose while the teapot hung over the fire on the end of a burning-stick. The sun warmed us and the wind ruffled our hair. How could a reasonable man wish for anything more?

We coasted along for twelve more miles down the meandering river. The left bank was low and marshy, but the right bank was steep and sandy and forty to fifty feet high. It was gradually being cut away by the river, and was littered with trees that toppled as the soil was washed from under them. Other trees were in various stages of being destroyed by the river; they leaned out at crazy angles, some of them horizontal but still hanging on by a few roots.

As we relaxed by the fire after dinner, John said that it was one of those times when he wanted a cigarette so that he could "burn the taste of the food out of my mouth." Now there is an odd reason for smoking! If I had my druthers, I would select a snifter of brandy or some other elixir. Rather than noxious fumes in my lungs, I would prefer something to mellow my soul and enhance my dreams.

After wading the long rapids we stopped on a pristine beach and boiled the kettle.

July 29

ANOTHER FINE DAY. By noon we had covered the twelve miles to the head of our last rapids on the Taltson. We saw another moose, but we certainly couldn't be bothered with more fresh meat. For several miles before the rapids the river went through country that had been burned over within the past few years—recently enough so that birch trees had not yet made a fresh start. The ridges and slopes were blanketed with carmine fireweed; quite a pretty tapestry if one could ignore the sad ugliness of a bare, blackened forest remnant.

Tall spruce on a huge sand hill.

Our last rapids was a long one—perhaps half a mile with a drop of twenty-five feet. It looked as if the wading might be good, so although it was past noon we postponed lunch until we reached the bottom. But we were deceived. The wading turned out to be abysmally bad. Most of the rocks were slime-covered, there were many sudden drop-offs and obstructing boulders, and two-thirds of the way down we reached an impasse. The water became too deep and swift for wading, so we had to unload and carry our gear across 150 feet of jumbled boulders in the river bed. Negotiation of the entire rapids took nearly three hours. We felt weak and faint; we had had no food since breakfast. We paddled a short distance and stopped for lunch at 4:30. The cooked strips of meat had gone bad. They were raising a crop of white maggots and giving off a fearful stench.

Landing place on a rocky island.

We rested for more than an hour, then paddled up the lake and camped on a rocky island. The fresh meat was high, but not so far gone that we couldn't have it for one more meal. John cut the pieces to bite size, and we fried them thoroughly. The remainder of the meat, about five or six pounds, we dumped in the lake. We had fourteen meals of fresh moose and three meals of the cooked stuff. The cooked meat was a disappointment because it didn't last longer, but we couldn't spare the time to prepare it properly.

Alone at last

We had been out seven weeks from the Black Lake post—about two-thirds of the trip gone by. Had we met anyone in that empty, lonely land we would have been surprised—and somewhat annoyed. We had grown accustomed to having the world to ourselves, and had no inclination to change the arrangement. Having other people about would have upset the balance of nature. And I, for one, would have been fearful. Had a stranger suddenly appeared I automatically would have regarded him as a potential enemy, someone up to no good and assumed to be guilty of evil intent until proven innocent. I can't explain it; it was simply how I felt. Perhaps such an isolated existence tends to make one paranoid. The vast, impersonal wilderness was implacably opposed to us; any mistake we made would be magnified tenfold by our distance from civilization. We had traveled so long and come so far into the heart of emptiness that we were beginning to wonder whether the rest of the world truly existed. It had been at least two weeks since we had seen or heard an airplane, and forty-six days since our last human contact.

Already some of our discussions were about what we would do in the interval between getting to Snowdrift and the time John had to be home to take up his teaching job. The first problem would be to arrange for transportation from Snowdrift to Yellowknife to Edmonton. From there we would drive west to Jasper National Park and south to Lake Louise and Banff. Then, if time permitted, west again to Vancouver and Seattle before calling it a season. Whatever was over the next hill, and the one beyond that, kept pulling us on.

Blueberries

July 30

THE FAIR WEATHER still held. We always began a day in high spirits when the sky was blue and the air was still. Shortly after we set out we spotted two moose feeding in the grass on the north shore of the lake. We weren't interested in eating them and they wouldn't let us get close enough for pictures, so on we went. We paddled for an hour and a half on the lake, then started up a narrow winding channel through grassland. After only a third of a mile the channel ended, and the course of the stream went sharply uphill and became quite rocky. John spent two hours reconnoitering to see if there was a place upstream where we might put in again, but no such luck. There were too many boulders, and not enough water to do a week's laundry, much less float a canoe.

John was gone so long that I became quite worried, and had difficulty quelling a surge of panic. My mind conjured up all the worst possibilities. What if John fell and broke an ankle? Or fractured his skull? Worse yet, what if he never returned? I tried to think calmly of what I would do if the worst came to pass, but the gears in my mind refused to mesh and I got nowhere. When John came plodding back he was surprised to hear that I'd been worried, and I was more relieved than I could express. I would have been mighty lonely out there all by myself.

What, me worry?

With a long portage facing us we decided the time had to come to abandon one of our boxes. We unloaded onto some rocks at the foot of the rapids, and spent two hours repacking. We placed the box on a boulder by the bank about three feet above water level, which should have been high enough to keep it from being swept away by the spring flood. The place was almost exactly on the sixty-second parallel. On the underside of the lid we printed our route and signed our names.

Carrying plywood to the North. We abandon one box.

Carrying on

It was too late in the day to do the entire portage, so we carried a mile and camped for the night. Even though we had abandoned the box we still had six loads, but the average weight was of course much less than at the beginning of the trip; the box itself weighed seventeen pounds. With more repacking we would have it down to five loads in a day or two. On the second carry John shot a grouse, which tasted good after a long day. It was 7:30 by the time we finished carrying, and the no-see-ems and mosquitoes were hitting us hard. We ate a late meal and went straight to bed, leaving our gear in disarray.

July 31

WE PORTAGED for a mile and a half to start the day. On that portion of the route we were relying almost entirely on aerial photos. We were headed north, hopping along a succession of ponds and small lakes on our way to Eileen Lake and the beginning of the Snowdrift watershed.

The portage took a lot out of us. We finished it at 2:00 and had a lunch of beans, tea, and two spoonfuls of marmalade each, which finished the can. There were just two cans of preserves left. We paddled across a small, shallow pond of intensely dark blue water entirely surrounded by boulders. It was a place of harsh, pure beauty—naked and clean, like the world when it was young. We portaged half a mile to the next minuscule lake, where we camped. It was an exhausting day; we pushed ourselves to the limits of our strength. I marveled that flesh and bone could endure such punishment.

I could easily understand how, in circumstances such as ours, a man might come to resent or hate his partner. There was no escape from the presence of the other, and no release from the exacting demands of the life. Absorbed in one's own privations, it was easy to forget that the other man was in the same predicament. Suspicion, mistrust, and recrimination lay just beneath the surface, and once set free would destroy you.

Proper canoeists

John and I protected ourselves by the instinctive use of a simple strategy. We were mindful of the other's troubles, we were solicitous, and we said "please" and "thanks."

No matter that our table manners had deteriorated, that our clothes were filthy, that our bodies were rank. We were still civilized in the most important sense of the word.

August 1

THE SUMMER MONTH of August came in like early November in more southerly altitudes: windy, cool, misting rain. We started the day with a one-mile paddle, followed by a portage of four-tenths of a mile to a lake that offered some four miles of actual canoeing again. It was quite a novelty. With all that portaging we felt like cross-country furniture movers.

We were beginning to wonder whether our food would last. Fish, fowl, and game were very uncertain; either they were present in great numbers or were totally absent. Blueberries were beginning to ripen and were plentiful in many places, but we had not yet discovered anything else edible in that land.

On the open part of the lake the wind kicked up ever larger waves. We tacked this way and that, but couldn't make it no matter what we did. It became dangerously rough, and we were blown onto the western shore, where we huddled under a tarp, built a fire to brew tea, and had our lunch.

Childhood revisited

The wind continued, so we wandered about, eating blueberries. It was haphazard at first, but soon we made a concerted effort and eventually managed to pick a quart. It was like a return to childhood: carefree, random activity, and no consciousness of time. Two grown, bearded men, pots and cups in hand, raincoats flapping in the wind, traipsing across patches of tundra and outcroppings of bedrock on an afternoon of blueberry picking. I was uncomfortable because of the cold damp wind, yet I felt exhilarated. Time stood still for an afternoon, and we were free—free of cares, of worries, of responsibilities, of the need to do work. As soon as we comprehended that we were free, why naturally we played.

At 4:00 the wind let up enough for us to get away, so we were obliged to get back into harness. We paddled to the north end of the lake, portaged 200 feet, and paddled 2,000 feet more to the beginning of the next portage. We unloaded onto tundra, and carried the tent and cooking gear a hundred yards inland to the nearest firm, level ground. We set up a lean-to and got under it, feeling thankful for its meager protection. Even when it wasn't drizzling or misting, the lean-to gave us a fine sense of security; it was almost like having four walls and a roof. In such a fashion did we deceive ourselves. It was a soggy, dismal evening.

August 2

THE WEATHER could hardly have been less encouraging—a solid low overcast, an occasional sprinkle, and a raw east wind. But we dutifully packed up and started out; there was no time to waste. We portaged 1,200 feet to the next pond. Beginning with the second carry the rain came down in earnest. That, in conjunction with walking over soggy tundra and through wet bush, soon had us soaked to the thighs. Our feet gradually became damp even though we were wearing waders, for water ran down our pants and socks and into our boots.

Where we put the canoe into the water at the end of the portage, there were a dozen rotting birch poles half buried in the mud. We pulled them out and used them as a ramp for launching the canoe over some rocks—the purpose for which they had been cut long ago.

John with the canoe on a cold and dreary August day.

We paddled a mile up the pond in a driving rain. By then we were looking for a spot to erect a lean-to for an early lunch and a temporary truce with the weather. We found none where we unloaded, so we portaged 600 feet to the next pond. The wind grew stronger and brought with it bursts of icy rain. The combination made portaging across exposed terrain as difficult and uncomfortable as canoeing under the same conditions. When John carried the canoe I had to walk in front of him and hold the bow so that he would not be toppled or have the canoe picked off his shoulders by the wind. We were soaked through, shivering, and thoroughly miserable by the time we finished the third carry.

Cold and wet

We put up a lean-to on a steep, mostly bare slope, got a hot fire going, and had a lunch of beans, "pemmican," and tea. Our so-called pemmican bore no relation to the original, which consisted of desiccated lean meat pounded into a powder, mixed with the fat of the same animal, and pressed into cakes, which would keep for a long time. What we had was a latter-day canned version, prepared by a California firm as an emergency ration for survival kits. It had a dense, fruitcake consistency, packing 407 calories into a three-and-a-half-ounce can. The main ingredients were seedless raisins, peanuts, and evaporated apples—quite a tasty dish. The lunch—what there was of it—was delicious, and we could easily have eaten four times as much.

The wind switched around to the north, and the temperature fell into the low thirties. We decided to stay put, and offered up a prayer for something better on the morrow. We spent the rest of the day huddled under the lean-to, except for erecting the tent, wood-gathering, and John picking three cups of blueberries in late afternoon. For a while we hashed over some topics we had covered from all angles previously: marriage versus the nomadic life, the unwillingness of either of us to be tied down to a nine-to-five slow death, and so on and so forth. But at the moment we could sure appreciate the advantages of settled home life. In fact, we could see the advantages of doing almost anything other than what we were doing. It was on such days that I wished I had never gone on that trip. In looking over the past eight weeks, all I could remember were eternally gloomy weather and an endless succession of exhausting struggles, and when I considered the remainder of the trip I couldn't imagine that it would improve. Perhaps there is a Gresham's Law concerned with isolation and travel in the wilderness: bad days invariably drive out the good. Yet even in those periods of

Gloomy

despondency induced by foul weather, weariness, and a mounting intellectual stagnation, we were aware that the journey had one major, saving aspect: action. We needed action that had a goal, a purpose, however ephemeral it might turn out to be, and that from time to time provided a fresh experience. Our normal lives, for all their interests and diversions, were too often consumed in meaningless motion and lost in experiences repeated so often they had degenerated to mere sensation. The vacuity that characterizes

Keep going on

most lives—ours included, at times, I am sorry to say—is not indefinitely bearable. Eventually one has to make a move. Action is all.

August 3

WE OVERSLEPT and didn't get under way until 10:00 on the final day of wearisome portaging. The morning consisted of two short portages of about 250 yards each, separated by short paddles of ten to fifteen minutes. We had lunch at the beginning of the half-mile portage to Eileen Lake.

We were listless after eating. The sun had been out only briefly; most of the time it was hidden behind a thin cloud layer. John again theorized that we were not getting enough

Author with hundred-pound load, approaching Eileen Lake—the tenth portage in five days.

food to keep us going full blast. He might have been partly right, but I still leaned toward the psychological theory. That was the tenth portage in five days, an arduous grind made all the more difficult because we had a good idea of what was coming up.

We trudged over the portage and reached Eileen Lake at last, only two days late on our schedule. The sky was slowly clearing again, and there wasn't much wind. It was cold all day, even when the sun was shining. We had to wear gloves while paddling.

Author protecting our gear from harm. The campsite on Eileen Lake.

Eileen Lake was the beginning of the Snowdrift watershed. It was all downhill from there on. The only obstacles would be rapids and the increasing possibility of bad weather. We paddled along the right shore of the lake and stopped on a long curving beach backed by tall trees, a choice campsite after five straight nights of rocky ground. Our approach to shore was heralded, as usual, by a greater yellowlegs sandpiper. Yellowlegs took the role played by blue jays back in the Banana Belt. At our appearance, a yellowlegs invariably perched atop the tallest tree, crying endlessly and raucously, informing the entire North that dangerous intruders had arrived.

Sentinel of the North—
a greater yellowlegs sandpiper.

Both of us had discovered, and would readily admit, that neither the reality of crashing through the bush, conquering nature, and overcoming all odds, nor the abstract image of ourselves doing those things, any longer pleased us the way it once did. Perhaps that changed feeling signified a certain kind of maturity—or encroaching age. The mystique of the wilderness was gone, too. We saw it as common rather than exotic, and didn't give it attributes it didn't have.

Utopian dreams

In our utopian dreams we might have wished to stay in the wilderness forever, but it was much too late for that. We had been refined and corrupted by our culture; a return to simplicity and innocence was no longer possible. The many aspects of civilization beckoned, and could not be ignored or refused forever. The only realistic hope was that we would not be engulfed by them.

The sense of living inside an embracing nature comes to a halt in the individual who has achieved it. With the best will and the finest intentions in the world, this palpable feeling had not been passed on to us by the many thousands gone before; nor would we be able to transmit it to all those who had stayed at home, or to those yet to come. We grew older and more blasé, but at times we could still recapture the feeling of overwhelming awe, the ecstasy and the rapture, at being surrounded by a wondrous world, with our survival depending entirely on our own efforts. It is a feeling never evoked, and seldom even imagined, by those who live in the technological milieu. We had come a great distance and made an extreme effort to attain it. I cannot answer if this was to the good. We were desperate to escape the confines of our civilization, and now that we had escaped we were becoming desperate to return. One might say with Thoreau: "It is a characteristic of wisdom not to do desperate things." But was

Thoreau said . . .

there any choice? We had been unable to find the middle ground.

Even when enraptured we were conscious that the environment was hostile and pitiless; we had best make tracks for Snowdrift. By sundown the sky was clear, there was not a breath of wind, the lake was calm, and another cold night was in store.

August 4

I PASSED A VERY COLD and interminable night. No one who has spent a night being continuously cold will forget the experience. One waits in hopeless despair for the first sign of light, the first sun ray, the least trace of warmth.

It was a clear cool morning with a gentle breeze, a perfect day for traveling. By midmorning we passed the line on the map that read: "Approximate northernmost limit of trees," and we were then in the Barrens. There were still many small trees in areas with good water and sheltered from the prevailing winds, but most of the country was treeless. It grew grasses, lichens, and low stunted bushes, including those delicious blueberries. We had a view for many miles to a horizon of gray, green, brown, and blue, with an occasional lone thin tree silhouetted against the sky. The Barrens had an austere and rugged beauty that was more appealing than the confining forest wall. That is, with the sun shining. When it was overcast, cold, and raining horizontally, it presented a grim and inhospitable scene.

The Barrens

Although no one has been able to pinpoint many of the lakes on Hearne's route, it is possible that Eileen Lake is the "Clowey Lake" of his day. Hearne spent two and a half weeks at Clowey Lake in May of 1771, and wrote: "It is a famous collecting-place for Indians proceeding to the barren ground, for it is the last place with good woods about it, and it is here that they halt to build their canoes." But that was long ago. No one goes there during the summer any more, and we did not know if the Indians traveled that far afield in winter. We had seen no signs.

Edge of the Barrens

August 5

WE STOPPED at the head of a short rapids for a lunch of cold fried fish, bread and peach jam, and tea. After lunch we ran the rapids, then took a ten-minute hike up a nearby ridge whence we had a magnificent prospect of 360 degrees of country. There were lakes and rivers and long low hills; the farthest ridges were thirty or forty miles off. We could see two long, violent rapids on the Eileen River, with the possibility of more beyond. As usual when we wandered about on shore those days, we spent many minutes picking and gobbling blueberries. Idyllic moments flitted away in the warm sunshine, with the sweet taste of the berries in our mouths and the virgin scenery a joy to our eyes.

But back to the business of getting down the river. Half a mile downstream we came to the first of the two rapids. There was a drop of fifteen feet in a series of cascades too rough to be waded, so we had to make a quarter-mile portage. It was very slow going, since we simply lacked the energy. Then there was a short paddle to the next rapids, which required a portage of about 350 yards over boulders. We were so run-down that it took a great effort just to walk back for the next load. A decent campsite offered itself at the end of the portage, and we gratefully seized it. We needed twenty minutes of complete rest before we even felt up to erecting the tent.

Idyllic moments

"There were lakes and rivers and long low hills . . . ."—and blueberries.

August 6

In the interest of eating a large breakfast we sacrificed some time, but food loosened our tongues the way alcohol does in the Banana Belt, and we had a good conversation. We talked ourselves into better spirits, and started out with considerable vigor.

We portaged once in the morning, and spent most of the afternoon up to our knees in water, wading down two rapids. Then a short paddle brought us to the last rapids before Tent Lake, which we could see spreading out beyond the narrows, with the late afternoon sun throwing a glistening silvery streak across the water. The rapids was about seventy-five yards long with a number of those swooping waves that swamped us several weeks ago, but we decided to run it. We shipped a few gallons of water; nothing serious, but we confessed to each other later that we both had expected to be swamped. As soon as we were out of the rapids we cut to the left and unloaded onto a fine sandy beach for the night, even though it was only five o'clock. The wind had been strong from the east all day, and crossing Tent Lake was out of the question.

John on an island in Eileen Lake. "Approximate northernmost limit of trees."

My ability to exist at close quarters with John had increased considerably since the early days of the trip when I was often annoyed by his personal habits. Now I scarcely noticed them. I was more sensitive to his moods, and had greater consideration for the needs and desires that moved him to act as he did. Our lives had blended quite well; it was, in fact, our differences in temperament and personality that made it so. It might not have turned out like that had I made the trip with another Peter Browning or he with another John Blunt. The pressures of living in the bush with only one or two companions have been too much for many men to handle. There are grim stories of those whose minds became inflamed against their partners, and often the result was murder and suicide.

I did not know if we would remain close friends when we got on the Outside again, but that was of no concern to me then. If a man has one good friend at a time, he is supplied with all the friendship he needs.

The last rapids before Tent Lake. Every rapids had to be scouted, no matter how safe it looked from above. This one had standing waves three feet high.

August 7

THE WEATHER, deceptively calm at our sheltered campsite, was not at all calm on the lake. A brisk wind from the south was kicking up large swells and whitecaps. We tacked several times, and after forty-five minutes of hard paddling and some anxious moments we reached the lee of an island where we put ashore to puzzle out our exact location and take a closer look at the waves before setting out again. As the trip wore on we were less inclined than ever to take chances. Certainly we wanted no repetition of our experience on McArthur Lake, when the waves came within a hair's breadth of doing us in.

Our course was west-northwest through a profusion of islands, and we weren't able to determine exactly which one we were on. We hopped half a mile to another island where we had lunch—the last of the bread and jam. For the past four days we had been piling jam on our bread in prodigious amounts—huge gobs of jam heaped onto and running over the sides of minute chunks of bread. Thereafter we would have a can of pemmican apiece for lunch, except on chocolate-bar days, until it ran out. And then? Perhaps a fish or duck would happen our way and keep us eating for the last few days.

Jam today; no jam tomorrow

Often we felt that we were the only inhabitants of a deserted planet.

After lunch we hopped half a mile to another island. We were deceived once again by water that appeared calm; a short distance from land the water was rough, and we had quite a struggle to reach solid ground again. This third island was barren, but we chose to sit it out until the wind abated. We decided the afternoon could be well spent picking blueberries for the pie John planned to bake with the last of the flour, so we sallied forth with pot and cup. The berries were sparse and it was a very cold job since the best picking was on an exposed ridge, but we kept at it until we had a quart.

Let them eat pie

As soon as the wind and waves seemed to have lessened, we headed for the southern outlet of the Eileen River. When

Author with map. Where do we go from here?

Somewhere in Tent Lake. John on the highest ground with map and compass, looking for the route.

we were halfway there we were out of the lee of the island and being shoved along at a furious rate by a strong wind and huge swells. It was not possible to tack, so once again we were in danger and forced to run before the wind to wherever it would take us. This had happened so often that I couldn't get excited—only annoyed because I was cold and wet from an occasional splashing wave. The wind blew us into the northern outlet, three-quarters of a mile above where we wanted to be. There was only a thin stream of water falling abruptly over a five-foot drop and winding away through a rocky, unnavigable channel. We would have to portage.

It was a rotten place to camp, but we had no choice. We unloaded onto a slab of rock, and carried the tent fifty yards up a slope to find level ground. We ate, and turned in at ten thirty with the wind still howling.

August 8

THE WIND blew from the south all night. A thin haze was partly obscuring the sun when we arose, and there was a distinct possibility of showers blowing up later in the day.

Growing old graciously

We started the day by portaging a quarter of a mile, always a bad way to begin. We had our gear down to five loads; the fifth was only a partial load at that. It consisted of the two sleeping bags, the tarps, tent and fly, and sometimes a rifle. After carrying the box I took my packframe back and strapped all the loose gear to it for the odd carry. We had lifted, carried, heaved, and dragged our canoe and various pieces of baggage innumerable times. We certainly needed the contents of the baggage, but often it seemed like an incubus on our backs. We were becoming the Old Men of the Inland Seas, bowed down and aged before our time by the weight of self-inflicted burdens—the history of the human race in a nutshell.

On the shores of the Inland Seas.

Rain fell off and on during the morning. Twice we pulled to shore and sat under a tarp until it stopped. Just after lunch we came to a waterfall with a drop of about twenty-five feet. What with the bad weather and our general fatigue, we decided to call it a day. We put up a lean-to at a slow, dragging pace interspersed with much blueberry picking. In the evening we walked over what would be the next morning's portage to see what it was like. Near the end of it we ran across an Indian winter camp; there were many cut trees and a large fire area. We found thirty-eight .303 cartridges, twenty of them still in their box. Probably they were dropped in deep snow by their owner, who was then unable to find them. We took them with us and would attempt to barter them for food at Snowdrift.

Very tired. All I could think about were food and sleep.

August 9

WE HAD A DAY of short portages and wading down rapids, and in late afternoon camped on a beach—our best campsite in a week. The map indicated an intermittent stream from this point to the next lake and the continuation of the river, but we could find no trace of it. We had the feeling that the cartographer, thinking that the river *must* go through, but unable to see it on the aerial photo, arbitrarily drew a dotted line on the map. Not only was there no sign of a stream, but there was actually a three-hundred-foot-high ridge beginning directly back of our campsite. In the evening we hiked up onto the ridge, which was broad and flat on top, and walked until we could see the next lake. There was going to be a long portage—about a mile and a half.

After the dishes were washed we sat by the fire and stared into the flames. Our talk turned obsessively to the Outside, in particular to that large chunk of real estate south of the forty-ninth parallel. Our conversation that evening was

Economism

concerned with the nearly total dominance in the United States of "economism" as a social philosophy. Economism is that attitude that interprets the whole sum of human existence in terms of the production, distribution, and acquisition of wealth. It is economism that drives America toward its goals: increase the number of things, develop the capacity to move larger objects and more people from one place to another at ever greater rates of speed, and expand the economy—forever. Matter is the dreadful burden of the modern era: matter collected, worshipped, and sped on its way to an unimaginable future.

How incredibly inane to spend one's life producing and consuming. We were already convinced of that, but now it was even more obvious. Each mile farther north and each additional day of a simple, uncluttered life brought us a bit closer to a sort of vantage point. We looked back at what we had left, and found it both ludicrous and sad. It was difficult to believe that it had actually become what it is—a bizarre, kaleidoscopic collection of paltry ambitions and inhuman goals. John and I would do well to escape such a fate, even should we never achieve anything else. Snowdrift was our goal, and our only ambition was to keep from being swept away by the torrent of modern life.

Ludicrous and sad

Samuel Hearne, in his journal, gave his views on the difference between the Indians who gathered many furs and traded at the Hudson's Bay Factory, and those who lived off the land by doing only as much as necessary and never, in effect, attempting to acquire a surplus. Of the former he said that "those who endeavor to possess more, are always the most unhappy, and may, in fact, be said to be only slaves and carriers to the rest." And of the latter he said, they "live generally in a state of plenty, without trouble or risque; and consequently must be the most happy, and, in truth, the most independent also. It must be allowed that they are by far the greatest philosophers, as they never give themselves the trouble to acquire what they can do well enough without."

Hearne said . . .

Well, we bought and sold nothing today, produced no trinkets, consumed nothing but food, and were four miles farther from the boundaries of economism.

August 10

I AWOKE shortly before six thirty, counted the days, determined that it was the tenth, and announced to John: "Today is a chocolate-bar day." Although it seemed like precious little to look forward to, it probably would be the pinnacle of the day. The scope of our lives was so narrow and the range of our interests had become so limited that a bit of chocolate filled our thoughts to the exclusion of all else.

Perhaps Freud was wrong after all. Had he ever gone into the bush for a few weeks he would have realized that it is food that is the motivation of all human thought and action. Just think how American society would benefit from such a

But Freud didn't say . . .

revelation! Food obsessions are ever so much more socially acceptable than sexual drives. Or perhaps it was simply that John and I were masters at sublimation. With tongue in cheek I tried out my theory on John. He was skeptical. But the truth was that for us, there and then, sex meant nothing, intellectual matters meant nothing, entertainment and diversion meant nothing. Food may not have been the only thing in life, but it was miles ahead of whatever was in second place.

Using the canoe as a windbreak. It didn't do much good.

With a long portage facing us, including a stiff climb to the top of the ridge, we decided to condense everything into four loads no matter how heavy they might turn out to be. We got going with our packs at ten thirty, and made it to the top before we took our first break. Again we were blessed with good weather—a bit on the cool side and somewhat windy on the exposed ridge, but sunny all day. It was like Indian summer in the Midwest arrived two months early. But we were out of the Barrens and had better protection from the wind, since the treeline slanted off to the northwest.

Shortly past noon we reached the lake and headed right back for the second load, having resolved not to eat lunch until the portage was finished. The second carry—John with the canoe and I with the box—was not as tough as anticipated. We rested once when we were three-quarters of the way up the ridge, and then made it the remainder of the way nonstop. We sustained ourselves with lemon drops while carrying the loads, and with quickly picked sprigs of blueberries while on the back trail. The second carry took an hour and twenty-five minutes, which wasn't bad for a couple of tired old men.

At three we got around to eating our well-deserved lunch—finishing it with those wonderful chocolate bars. We loaded up and started along the lake, and in an eighth of a mile we were wading down a long shallow rapids. Had there been a few more inches of water we could have run it with ease, but as it was we would have been scraping over rocks every few feet. We worked away at the wading for an hour and a half, but finally had to give it up and make camp on rocky ground. The rapids stretched on as far as we could see, and more wading was in store.

Seeing the light

John, who once bolted his food and scarcely seemed to taste it at all, had slowed his eating speed drastically and now relished every bite, while I, on the contrary, had speeded up in order to get the food eaten before it cooled. In the past, both of us had regarded eating as largely nothing more than a basic necessity and frequently an evil, a waste of important time. All that had changed. We had seen the light, and any expression of the former attitude was blasphemy. Eating was our chief delight: thoughts of food filled our days and haunted our dreams, and we mouthed every morsel with sensual pleasure.

August 11

PADDLING TOOK US a hundred feet downstream to start the day, and then we waded for the next two hours. The river was wide, shallow, and rocky; frequently we got hung up and had to backtrack. At last we came to a pond. It was only a few hundred feet across to the next constriction on the map, which we were certain would be another rapids, but to our delight we lucked out for a change. It was a narrow, rock-bound channel, but perfectly calm. Our morale improved so much that we broke into laughter and shouts of triumph and glee, and whipped out our cameras to snap a few pictures of each other and the quiet, still beauty of the spot. It sure didn't take much to make us happy.

Easily pleased

During the afternoon we paddled three miles, portaged 200 yards around a rapids, and camped on a narrow strip of rocky ground at the head of another rapids. John scouted the portage we would make first thing the next morning, and while at the foot of the rapids did some fishing. He brought back three grayling, which would do for breakfast and lunch the next day, when we hoped to reach the Snowdrift.

August 12

ANOTHER DAY of perfect weather. We knocked off the portage, waded a short rapids, crossed a small lake, and came to the head of the last rapids on the Eileen River. It was at least three-quarters of a mile long and much too rough to wade. We unloaded on the right bank and portaged through beautiful open park country across a great sand plain overlooking the foaming Eileen and its confluence with the Snowdrift, which wound away between sandy banks and low forested ridges. It was the northernmost point of the trip, approximately 62° 32′ North Latitude. From there the Snowdrift flowed west-southwest to Great Slave Lake—the homestretch at last.

Farthest north

We started down the Snowdrift, spotted a caribou at once, but he disappeared into the bush. Two miles farther on we saw another, a young buck who swam the river about a quarter of a mile ahead of us and began to graze on tall grass along the bank. We stopped paddling and floated silently down upon him. He saw us, but wasn't alarmed and continued grazing. The .270 was not accessible, but when we were about a hundred feet away John shot him twice with the .22—in the neck and the head—and he keeled over dead in his tracks. I set up camp on the opposite bank while John butchered him at top speed. From shooting to frying pan was about an hour and a half.

Killing and eating

Once again I felt badly about the killing of an animal. The caribou herds have been greatly depleted during the past century, at least in part because of the introduction of high-powered rifles. Even the most conservative estimates of caribou population indicate that before the arrival of white men the caribou numbered upward of three million, and that presently there are no more than three hundred thousand.

We were short of food, despite the addition of the caribou. The Dri Lite and the supply of shortening were dwindling, and we ran out of pepper several days earlier. Undoubtedly we would reach Snowdrift with a bare larder. We hoped we wouldn't be on short rations the last few days.

Weariness and Hunger

August 13

WE GOT UP EARLY, but didn't shove off until after ten because we had to cut up the caribou. It was a serene and lovely river. There were many sand bluffs eight to ten feet high, sand and mud bars at every bend, and long stretches of one bank or the other consisting entirely of deposited silt. The traveling was as easy as we had hoped, although the current was difficult to follow and occasionally we ran aground in shallow water and had to wade the canoe to the next dropoff.

In the past three weeks of incessant traveling the lunch periods had become our most relaxed times, and we eagerly anticipated them. There was nothing to do but feed the fire, brew our tea, and eat whatever cold food we had prepared at breakfast or the night before. It was the only time of day when we were inclined to talk very much. Of late there had been little opportunity for reading, and less desire. We had thoroughly explored each other's attitudes and opinions on all matters of interest. Also we had debated the affairs of the day at great length, and were acutely aware that our information was badly dated. The big outside world hadn't spoken to us since early June. Of course, it might have ceased speaking altogether. For all we knew, the Banana

Local concerns

Belt was radioactive by then. But even *that* wouldn't have aroused our interest in the "important" problems: we were too tired. And we became more parochial every day. Other than food talk, we were concerned almost entirely with how far? how long? when? The journey continued.

Even with the late start and a quitting time of five o'clock, we made about twenty-two miles. We camped on a silt bank, and followed our hallowed routine: consumed huge quantities of meat, then made our sluggish way to bed.

August 14

A REPLICA of the day before. Identical weather: clear and with a tailwind except when the river looped to the north. But even in the sun the wind was chilly; I wore a sweater and John two shirts most of the day. It was difficult to estimate the distance traveled, since the river made so many twists and turns. On our 1:250,000 map it was not possible to straighten it out mentally or to make an accurate measurement. By a conservative estimate we covered about thirty-five miles.

A serene and lovely river, winding between sand banks, through forests of black spruce.

Boredom was our greatest problem. The repetitive, mechanical act of paddling exhausted our minds. Conversation waned, and we traveled along in stifling silence. I pulled my paddle through the water, the seconds ticked away; I pulled again, the miles crept by. I was drowning in monotony.

We camped on another silt bank, but had grass and lichen-covered spots for the tent and fire. Unloading was difficult. Where there were large silt or sand deposits and a sloping beach rather than a vertical bank, there was not much current. Therefore to get to shore we had a stretch of shallow water followed by a wide mud flat before we reached solid ground. That evening the canoe stuck in the mud about thirty feet from the bank. We dragged it a few more feet and then waded our gear ashore through the muck.

No restraint

For dinner I whipped up a large order of mashed potatoes and gravy, plus a vegetable, to go with our caribou. We were usually lethargic while on our heavy meat diet, and although we knew were overdoing it we seemed incapable of cutting down. To our credit, however, we rationed ourselves to two or three panfuls of meat for breakfast and two for lunch. This was in contrast to the six or seven we had been having for breakfast, and the same number or even more we still had for dinner.

August 15

UP EARLY, and paddling down the lazy river once more by eight thirty. The river was the same as before. The weather was mostly overcast and chilly, but there was little wind and the clouds did not look as though they would produce rain.

Lunch was cold meat, pemmican, and tea. What little sugar remained we were saving for the pie John would bake whenever he had the time, and we had been using saccharine to sweeten our tea. As our craving for sweets grew we increased the number of tablets per cup, and were up to six. We had so much saccharine—3,000 tablets—that we felt we could afford to be extravagant. By way of an experiment we each had a cup of tea with fifteen tablets in it, and discovered, to our annoyance, that anything over five or six tablets wouldn't make the tea any sweeter.

How sweet is sweet?

An hour after lunch we reached Siltaza Lake. A light breeze came up, but it was at our backs and we started along the lake following the north shore. After a couple of hours of crawling across an expanse of open water I was ready to throw a fit: jump out of the canoe, smash my paddle, scream and curse—anything to break the spell of crushing monotony and boredom.

We covered at least thirty miles and camped at the beginning of the narrow part of Siltaza Lake, two or three miles from where the river began again. We came across a family of foxes—a mother and three cubs—on a sandy plain back of our camp. The mother took off into the bush at top speed, and the cubs dived back into their burrow. We moved to within twenty yards of the burrow and lay flat on the ground. Soon the cubs came out again, to sit beside the burrow and stare at us. Their innocence was matched by our benevolence: we meant each other no harm.

They sat at the lip of their burrow, motionless, as though posing for their portraits.

Obsessions

Even as we stuffed ourselves at the evening steak fry we had food obsessions. They were becoming more intense all the time. We ridiculed ourselves for being so helplessly in the grip of these obsessions, but no amount of kidding, self-analysis, or strong resolve to forget about food for a spell could free us from them. It was a strange and upsetting feeling to find that we could not direct and control our thoughts. I wound up all my determination and announced firmly that I wouldn't mention food again for the rest of the evening. John seconded the motion with great fervor, but in a

few minutes, and with us unawares, the topic cropped up again, in the form of that transcendent question: What would you most like to be eating at this very moment? John spoke longingly of sardines on butter-smeared white bread, and I countered with a salad: tomato, cucumber, lettuce, and avocado, liberally covered with roquefort dressing. Then we avidly discussed sandwiches and salads for a time, drooling over our favorites and dreaming up bizarre combinations.

Sardines

August 16

DURING THE MORNING we waded four short rapids, all of them just slightly too formidable to be run. After the fourth we reached a pond with a good beach, and dried our pants, socks, and boots while eating lunch on a hillock. The remaining chocolate bars were in fragments, and we attempted to match them as in a jigsaw puzzle. Great care had to be taken in such a delicate operation, since the bars loomed large in our lives. The river improved after lunch. We came to three rapids, and were able to run them. Shortly after the third we decided to camp on an attractive sand bluff on a small pond.

Chocolate

The "meat syndrome" had hold of us again. We both were very lethargic and without any reserve strength—or any strength at all. I still thought the problem was largely psychological. We were weary of the isolated existence and the constant travel. Mental stagnation and physical fatigue were taking their toll; ever-greater efforts of will were required to accomplish tasks that had not increased in difficulty.

Earlier in the day we remarked that we would never again undertake such a strenuous or lengthy journey; it was a once-in-a-lifetime affair. Also, we both felt that we were too old for this sort of thing. I was thirty-five and John was thirty-three. It was a better game for those in their early or mid-twenties. Should we wish to go to that part of the world again, and could manage the expense, we would be in favor of flying in to some remote lake with our complete outfit and three or four weeks' supply of food, and then flying out. That's the armchair approach, but one is not able to do it the pure, hard way forever.

Age is wisdom

Yes, it would be a better game for younger men, but where shall one find them? All the young men of my acquaintance are older than I—and have been for many years. Some of them verged on decrepitude even before they first shaved. They were ever anxious to hasten into the next stage of life before they had learned to savor the one they were in. After spending the requisite time in an institution of higher learning, they plunged headlong into business and the professions. And before they had an inkling of what was happening they found their lives mortgaged to the ulcerous, corrosive pursuit of money, power, and success. Most of them have long since forgotten that they even so much as dreamed of setting out along a different road. The few whose memories can still be awakened by envy or despair will answer that they would dearly like to strike out on some new course, but they can't afford to since they have too much time and effort invested in the attainment of their present undesirable positions. They cannot even see their way clear to break free for a summer. A strange sort of investment, I think, that has no growth and pays no dividends. However fearful they may be, I would nevertheless advise them to cash in their chips at once, and invest the proceeds in whatever dreams remain to them.

Strange choices

As we headed toward the campsite we had selected we spotted a black bear roaming along the shore, eating blueberries. *Our* campsite, and *our* blueberries. The wind was toward us and he didn't get our scent, so when we were about 200 feet from shore we shouted to scare him off. He didn't have the brains to be frightened, however—probably hadn't had any contact with men before. He charged into the lake and splashed through the shallows toward us, obviously with unfriendly intentions. We hastily paddled away, whereupon he stopped, stared at us for a few moments, and slowly returned to shore. John unlimbered the .22 and fired several shots in an attempt to run him off, but the noise and the spurts of sand at his feet didn't faze him. John said he would have to wing the bear to get rid of him, and fired another shot. The bear leaped all the way off the ground, then ran up the bank and out of sight. An instant later we heard him crash through some brush, followed in a moment by two gurgling groans, and then silence. Thinking we had a wounded and irate bear on our hands, we landed a couple of hundred feet along the shore from where we'd last seen him, got out both rifles, and cautiously went looking. We found him dead fifty yards from shore. John's shot had caught him just behind the shoulder, apparently through the heart. We certainly didn't need, or desire, more fresh meat, but decided to sample him anyway, neither of us ever having had bear meat. The brains were tasty—indistinguishable from caribou or moose. We

A bad ending

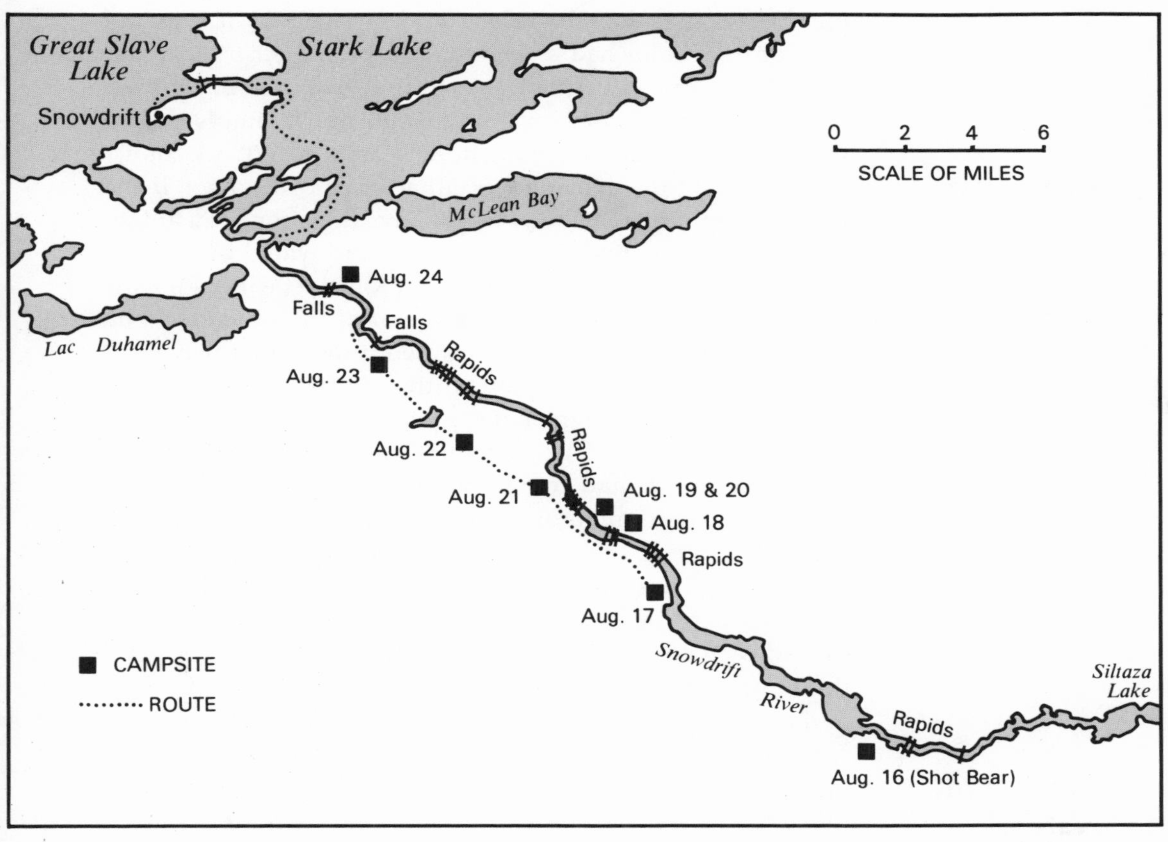

Great Slave Lake
Stark Lake
Snowdrift
0 2 4 6
SCALE OF MILES
McLean Bay
Aug. 24
Falls
Falls
Lac Duhamel
Rapids
Aug. 23
Aug. 22
Rapids
Aug. 21
Aug. 19 & 20
Aug. 18
Rapids
Aug. 17
Snowdrift River
Siltaza Lake
Rapids
Aug. 16 (Shot Bear)
CAMPSITE
ROUTE

also tried the liver and some cuts off a hindquarter. It was much too gamy for our civilized palates. Flesh and liver tasted remarkably alike, the only noticeable difference being the texture. The flesh was stringy, and tougher than caribou or moose. We ate only a few bites apiece, then threw away the rest and had caribou instead. Bear definitely is an acquired taste, although if we had been hungrier we surely would have acquired the taste at once.

John was somewhat shamefaced about killing the bear. Although we didn't hold with indiscriminate killing or killing for what is loosely referred to as "sport," it was my opinion that John had a tendency to be trigger-happy, and was all too ready to shoot at anything that moved. His explanation was: "I got him in my sights and I simply pulled the trigger without meaning to." It was a "gut reaction," which was all the explanation either of us could give. If the gun had been in my hands I might have done the same thing. But it did not matter whether we were motivated by hunger, by fear, or by some baser motive. To kill the bear or to let it live was not a question of principle or of moral values. The bear was an obstacle, and we wanted it out of the way. Had we given quiet consideration to the matter of how to deal with the bear we might have come up with a less deadly solution. But we had neither the time nor the patience for such niceties. We had come that far through the wilderness by means of determination and endurance. Our instincts had gradually forced their way to the surface, becoming more primitive and ferocious with the passage of time, and now we felt bound by few of the civilized restraints. John and I treated each other with respect, courtesy, and kindness, but I think we both were prepared to run roughshod over the rest of the world had it stood between us and our destination.

Instinctive men

Life on a level of bare subsistence, in competition with an indifferent nature, engenders a callousness to other life. I think this is true of most men, even those whose existence depends on abundant game and whose best interests dictate that they kill just what they need and no more. In the journal of his trip to the Coppermine, Samuel Hearne wrote that the Indians, upon encountering a large herd of caribou, would slaughter them wantonly and in some cases take only the tongues—considered a great delicacy—and leave all the rest to rot. They could not be made to understand that overkilling in the here and now might possibly make for a shortage in some other place at a later date. In the same context, Hearne

Indifferent Nature

wrote: "Indeed, they were so accustomed to kill everything that came within their reach, that few of them could pass by a small bird's nest without slaying the young ones or destroying the eggs."

And that, too, is in the bloodstream.

August 17

THERE WAS A RAPIDS within half a mile, but it was short and easily run. Before the day's travel had scarcely begun we were on Austin Lake and had eight or nine miles of open going to the beginning of the long series of rapids and falls leading to Stark Lake and Great Slave.

Signs of others

We paddled along steadily, stopping for fifteen minutes in midmorning to stretch our legs and pick blueberries. The berry season was about over; they were becoming shrunken and tart. When we stopped for lunch we found that we were getting back into well-traveled territory again. There were signs of old and recent camps, and a blazed tree with the year 1960 carved on it. We ate the last of the caribou and the last two tins of pemmican. The latter had become quite precious and eagerly awaited; we liked it even better than chocolate. It tasted like candy to us, and we nibbled it slowly to make it last through several cups of tea.

After lunch we paddled a mile and a half to the head of the next rapids. These rapids were of such a nature that there was no opportunity for wading. Rather than the even gradient that we had had on most previous rapids, the water dropped over rocky ledges, often three or four feet high. We stopped on the south bank and John went out to reconnoiter. He was gone two and a half hours, and returned quite weary from having clambered over rocks and crashed through the bush for most of that time. The rapids was much too long and rough to be either run or waded. John did not reach the end of it, and was discouraged because he had been unable to locate a portage route. But fifteen minutes before he returned he came upon a well-defined Indian trail that brought him back to where we had landed. It wasn't apparent from the landing, since the first hundred yards were over bare rock. We weren't certain of the length of the portage, but could only assume that it was a long one in order to bypass at least the first group of rapids.

Close by we found the remains of an old canvas canoe and many other worn-out articles discarded by the Indians:

rope, cans, rusted stovepipe sections. We were encouraged by the trash and by the trail, which led us to hope that there would be trails the rest of the way down the river.

Precious commodity

We ran out of salt that evening. For two days we had thumped the container with our knives to dislodge the solidified grains. When this no longer produced results we cut it open, scraped out the few remaining particles, and gloomily contemplated the prospect of unseasoned meals. As we took turns scraping out the last grains we watched each other like two prospectors weighing out gold dust—suspicious and greedy partners doing their level best to divide their treasure inequitably.

But it was of little importance. The day's work was finished, and we were at rest. Struggle and hardship were erased from memory. We were suspended at the center of a beautiful universe, and could believe that no one had ever seen those sights before. In that world that was so pristine and naive, and so heartless, one's own heart and mind were nothing. Nature was the only reality, and we had become an integral part of it.

Men on the Outside are constantly in conflict with nature, striving to subdue and exploit it. But for John and I to have assailed nature would have been an act of suicidal folly, akin to putting out our own eyes. For the sake of such a perfect harmony we gladly would have relinquished the transience and illusory brightness of our former existence. In life on the Outside it would seem we had mistaken the rind for the fruit itself.

The world was restless

The night was clear and mild. A deep black sky was strewn with stars. Directly overhead, in a course parallel with the river, the aurora cut a swath through the heavens—a long shifting streak of milky white and pale green, gossamer streamers of cool light falling toward the earth, flaring and fading, never still for an instant, always changing, trembling, swaying, undulating to a cosmic rhythm. I stared upward too long and was overcome by vertigo.

At our feet the fire also flared and faded. The black water of the Snowdrift slid past our rocky camp and shattered into phosphorescence in the rapids; smoke from the fire swirled away in the drifting air; the trees creaked and rustled in the dark. The world was restless. Everything was in flux, in motion.

The Long Portage

August 18

WE HIT THE TRAIL at eight o'clock sharp with the first of our two loads, after a breakfast of fruit, beans, and tea. The portions of beans were smaller than normal—half a dozen spoonfuls and they were gone. There had been no luck with the fishing recently, trout and jackfish being absent, and grayling hard to catch.

After several hundred yards of uneven, rocky terrain, the trail became good walking—mostly open park and sand plain. It was a long portage, about two and a half miles. At three o'clock we headed sharply downhill and at the same time sighted open water. The trail leveled off some distance above the river and ran parallel to it. We left the trail and

Self-deception

went straight downhill, forgetting, in our eagerness to be done with portaging, what had been demonstrated to us on many occasions and what we reminded ourselves of frequently: that the Indians were a practical people, that they did things in the easiest way possible and never expended more energy than necessary.

We had come past the first stretch of rapids, returning to the river a short distance above where a small tributary

entered from the south-southwest. We loaded down a steep, rocky incline, paddled ten minutes, and were at the next rapids. It was a short one, but the water dropped abruptly over a couple of ledges and we had to portage. We spent more than an hour looking on both sides of the river for a trail. We were unable to find the least trace of one, and couldn't figure out why the trail around the previous long stretch of rapids was so well defined yet dwindled to nothing half a mile downstream. We were frustrated and fatigued, so we camped on an attractive sand plain atop a fifteen-foot bluff on the north bank.

August 19

WE PICKED OUT a portage route around the rapids, paddled ten minutes to the next rapids, couldn't find a trail—no traces, no artifacts. The north bank was impassable because of steep ledges. After extensive scouting we picked out a route on the south side. We landed on a pile of jumbled rocks, then went steeply uphill to 100 feet above the river, and downstream over huge boulders. It was very slow and tricky going, and tiring as well.

No sooner had we carried our packs to the foot of the rapids than it began to rain. By the time we got back to the canoe it was almost impossible to stand on the slippery rocks. We sat on a flat rock and huddled under a tarp, gradually becoming more wet and miserable, and hoping the rain would blow over and we could continue. We ate a lunch of beans and chocolate bars under the tarp, and talked about the absence of signs of Indian life and the increasingly difficult portages.

Misery

I recalled an article that had appeared some years earlier in *The Beaver*, the house organ of the Hudson's Bay Company. It was written by Guy Blanchet who, with five others, went down the Snowdrift in 1925, sticking to the river all the way. The Indians had told him about an old portage trail, but

"I think maybe no"

though he kept a sharp lookout he could not find it. In the most difficult part of the river, which was still ahead of us, Blanchet and his party had many rough portages over rocky ledges, and frequently had to cross from one side of the river to the other in dangerous currents. In the worst stretch they spent three days making six miles. Blanchet did not think a canoe had been taken down the lower Snowdrift before, and he considered it unlikely that it would ever be attempted again. When his trip was finished, Blanchet remarked to an elderly Indian acquaintance that he had brought a canoe through the canyon of the Snowdrift. The old Indian thought it over, and replied: "I think maybe no."

We began to believe we had made a mistake in leaving the Indian trail the day before, although we found it almost impossible to entertain the notion that the trail went around all the rapids and falls. It would be easy enough to traverse by dogsled in winter, but it was a portage of monstrous proportions in summer. We spent more than three hours cringing under the tarp, growing wet, cold, and morose.

Rock bottom

That was the nadir of the trip. We were so down and out that we didn't even discuss food. Our minds refused to function. We were unable to reach a conclusion and embark on a course of action. If only some strong-minded, authoritative person had materialized and told us what to do we might have been able to get going again. It was those damned decisions that would kill us in the end.

Eventually we pulled ourselves together and decided that following the river with the loads we had was not feasible, and that we had best relocate the Indian trail and follow it without loads to determine where it went before committing ourselves to taking our outfit by any particular route. Wearily we clambered downstream over the boulders, brought back our packs, then paddled across the river to the only decent campsite we had seen. Retracing our steps was a big psychological blow. We were so depressed that we had to talk ourselves into performing our simple, routine tasks. "Let's set up the tent before we do anything else," I said.

When that was done John mentioned the next chore. "I guess we'd better scare up some dry wood," he said. "I guess so," I replied, and slowly, slowly we did that, too. We erected a lean-to and got a huge fire going.

Then we discussed the alternatives: get back on the trail and see where it would take us, follow the river, or—as an outside chance—explore the north bank of the river to see if the walking conditions were good. The first of the three looked like the best bet.

Snowdrift was only eighteen crow-fly miles away, but there was no telling how long it would take us to get there.

August 20

UP EARLY. Breakfast of beans and tea. Then upstream in the empty canoe. Over the previous day's short portage and back to where we had returned to the river when we left the trail. We found the trail again with no trouble, although it passed through an area where much camping had been done and was therefore indistinct. We started walking at seven thirty, stopping frequently to note the time and the direction of the trail and to check our approximate position on the map.

We lost the trail a few times during the morning, once for more than an hour. Finally we adopted the "straight-line" method and thereafter had no difficulty relocating the trail. In midmorning we came to four ponds surrounded by wiry brush and muskeg. The area was very swampy and the footing was terrible; several times we went in up to our knees. What a breeze it would have been in winter, making a straight line across the frozen ponds and the well-cut stretches of trail connecting them. But we had to crash and wade our way around each pond, clutching at the bushes and hauling our feet out of the sucking mud. I dreaded the thought of going that way with a load.

Dread anticipation

Beyond the ponds was a 200-yard-wide sand plain that had seen much camping. Many trees had been cut, the trail disappeared completely, and it took us half an hour before we could pick it up again. At noon we reached what at first we thought was the river, but our joy was short-lived. It turned out to be a small lake a mile and a half from the river. We bushwhacked our way around the lake and picked up the trail again on the other side. There we stopped for

lunch, such as it was: tea and half a bacon bar apiece. A bacon bar is equivalent to three-quarters of a pound of bacon. It is pre-fried, and sealed in heavy foil in a package three by one-and-a-half by one inches. The lunch was barely enough to make the saliva flow, but we were rationing the food because we were very short and didn't know how much longer we would be traveling.

Dieting

Our morale was at rock bottom. The trail gave no indication of heading for the river. The concept of a portage that length was overwhelming. A short walk after lunch brought us to two small ponds. We bushwhacked around both of them, finding the trail again with ease each time. Then we plodded on another mile and a half to another small lake, which had a distinctive shape and could be pinpointed on the map. The general direction of the trail was the same, approximately west-northwest—roughly parallel to the river and more than a mile from it. But if the trail continued in the same direction it might be headed for Lac Duhamel, southwest of Stark Lake and not where we wanted to go at all.

That was as far as we were able to follow the trail. We didn't have the time to go to the end of it since we had a long walk to get back to our camp and were without sleeping bags or provisions for spending a night out. We peered across that farthest lake, almost certain we could see where the trail began again on the other side. We decided that following the trail was the only way out, although just thinking about the immensity of such a portage fatigued and disheartened us.

Feeling low

At three we started back. We walked at a fast pace, making only one ten-minute stop after passing the four ponds, to empty water from our boots and wring out our socks. We reached the canoe at 6:45. We estimated the distance to the farthest lake at seven miles, with how much more we didn't know. We paddled downstream, walked over the short portage again, and were at our campsite by 7:30, hungry and tired.

August 21

A MINOR REPACKING in the morning. To lighten the loads we threw away an axe, John's packframe, the paddle we bought in Edmonton, and some odds and ends.

We started at ten o'clock. There was a short, hard paddle against the current, back over the same short portage, and to a sandy bluff at the mouth of the tributary. We ate a lunch of chili and tea, and then took off. The first part of the trail was sharply uphill, which took the wind out of our sails at once. We walked twenty minutes and then returned for the second load. There was a brief shower in the early afternoon, but in general the weather was good. There were no streams or ponds on that portion of the trail, so by the time the day, and we, were almost finished we had to camp on uneven ground near half a dozen stagnant pools of black swamp water.

John shot two grouse in midafternoon. Very tasty indeed, especially after a tough day. They also provided a badly needed supplement to our skimpy diet. I hoped we could keep going at full steam on such an abbreviated intake of food. We were hungry most of the time, but conscious not so much of hunger as of a general feeling of debility.

Peculiar thoughts

John remarked that rather than being forced to get along on reduced rations he would almost prefer to go without food entirely for a few days—just for the experience. I had had the same thought several times in recent weeks, but hadn't voiced it since it struck me as being grotesquely masochistic. My curiosity was aroused, though. How would our bodies perform after several days of no nourishment, and how would our minds function were we motivated solely by hunger? Life on the Outside will not permit any such revelations. The dwellers there, caught between dry routine and barren entertainment, are no longer moved by such questions. Their needs have been filled, and filled again; their first questions have been answered, and no new ones come to mind. Now there is nothing that can stir them. They are not impelled by curiosity, nor by hunger, nor even by the desire for freedom during one short season.

Under kinder circumstances John and I might have pushed this particular experience to its extreme. That is, if we hadn't been so hungry already we might have explored hunger more thoroughly.

August 22

UP AT FIVE and on the swampy trail at seven thirty. We flushed some grouse after the first five minutes. John spent half an hour going after them, and bagged three. We labored on through damp and muddy going. The toughest part of the morning was around the four ponds. We avoided them by making a wide loop to the south, but even there we encountered very bad conditions. There were a few thickly wooded patches and some water, but mostly muskeg and wiry bushes. We struggled through it, at times so bogged down in swamp and brush that it seemed we would not have the strength to take another dozen stumbling steps. When we reached the sand plain beyond the ponds after the second carry we were feeling nauseated from fatigue. But after a ten-minute break we got to our feet and went on; there was nothing else to do. Past the sand plain was a narrow stream in a six-foot-deep gully. We put the canoe in the water and floated the loads across one at a time. The banks were nearly vertical and were covered with unyielding bushes. It was difficult to wrestle the loads down the bank and into the canoe, but getting them up the other side almost whipped us. We mustered every ounce of strength, heaved them up with a convulsive effort, and half lunged, half fell after them so that they would not topple back upon us. We were left drained, limp, trembling.

Nausea

Fifteen minutes beyond the stream we stopped for lunch: beans and the last of the chocolate bars. We boiled swamp water for our tea. We could still afford to have a decent meal in the evening, but breakfasts and lunches were small. The portions of beans were half normal size—not even enough food for someone leading a sedentary life.

This was the worst ordeal we had ever experienced. At times on the trail I felt that it was all unreal, a nightmare. We were operating more on willpower than on actual strength. We *were* going to get out of there, we *were* taking all of our gear with us, we *were* going to finish the trip under our own power—and that's all there was to it. But I really wanted to become unconscious until that brutality was at an end.

Ordeal

By midafternoon we reached the first lake and crossed it. It was nice to be paddling again, however briefly, but the effort of loading and unloading the canoe took its toll and left us feeling weaker yet. We went to the first of the two small ponds and camped in a place much used by Indians. Their winter camps were obvious: trees were cut off at waist level, which was snow level when they were there. It looked as though a war had passed through, leaving only the splintered remnant of a forest. The delicious grouse partly revised us, but we were very tired and ready to turn in as soon as we finished eating.

August 23

We crossed the two ponds—two loadings and two unloadings. It felt like a full day's work. Then a long walk to the farthest lake we had reached three days earlier. It seemed like eons before.

En route to the lake John shot a grouse and a squirrel. We reached the lake at two o'clock, crossed it, and picked up the trail with ease. It was good walking and led northward toward the river. We were much encouraged but refrained from cheering. We hated to raise our hopes and risk having them dashed by an adverse development. About six o'clock we came upon a small stream of clear and very cold water, and at the same time we could see the Snowdrift River in the distance.

Eating squirrels

John shot another squirrel, so we had one apiece and half a grouse each for dinner. The squirrels were a bit gamy but perfectly edible; they had the texture and taste of duck. It was hard work to get the little bit of meat off the bones. Five or six squirrels would have been a decent ration for one man.

We were constantly hungry. Each dish tasted better than it ever had before, even without seasoning. Most foods definitely tasted sweet. For the past five nights we had had large servings of cabbage, an item we had in oversupply. We had tried cabbage the second night of the trip; both of us disliked it and swore never to eat it again. But now it not only came in handy but actually tasted good. We sprayed it with lemon concentrate, and it turned out somewhat like sauerkraut.

Eating cabbage

I dug out a book after dinner, but couldn't work up any interest in it. I had lost the ability to focus my thoughts. The book went back in the pack, I got into my sleeping bag, closed my eyes, and waited for oblivion.

August 24

THE FIRST THING we did each morning was to peer anxiously at the sky, hoping there was no rain in sight. We were up early, and the fair weather was still with us.

For breakfast we had scrambled eggs, the last of that commodity. It was a welcome change from the monotony of beans and chili, but even less feeling. We ate the last of the fruit and cooked up the last small batch of beans for lunch; the chili had been finished off the day before. At both breakfast and lunch for the past week we had been filling our bellies with numerous cups of tea. It gave us a feeling of satiety that lasted for about an hour.

Downgrade

The trail was either downgrade or level, all of it solid footing—a good thing, since we didn't feel up to doing anything more difficult. We crossed several broad sand plains dotted with tall trees. Each carry left us feeling a bit more apathetic and weak, even the downhill portions. The most tiring part was going back uphill for the second load.

Worn down

We stretched the final leg of the portage to thirty minutes because the river was so near. Toward the end of the second carry I nearly collapsed. I labored through the last twenty feet of muskeg, and had difficulty staying upright. I stumbled and weaved, my legs quivered and almost buckled, but I got squared away and kept going, and finally we were at the river. It was 1:30, seventy-two hours since we began the portage. We estimated the distance at thirteen miles, not counting the initial two and a half miles we did before leaving the trail and taking to the river again. It was enough portaging to last us forever.

For lunch we had the remnant of the beans, with one of the two remaining bacon bars by way of celebration. The river was broad and shallow—swift but smooth current interspersed with mild rapids. We waded part of the time, and ran down when the water was deep enough. We reconnoitered simply by looking ahead and deciding that it appeared okay. There was much scraping of the bottom. We were too tired to take our normal safety precautions or to care if the canoe acquired more scratches and dents.

If our figuring was correct, we had returned to the river below all the rapids but above the two falls that had portages designated on the map. At four o'clock we reached a falls with a drop of ten feet.

Although it was not late, we were too weak and weary to go on. After we landed I lay on my back on the rocks. I felt faint, and my stomach was so empty that my navel seemed to be hitting my backbone. We made camp on the spot, and left the short portage for the morning.

"There's no sauce in the world like hunger"

We had a large dinner. The entrée was the can of two freeze-dried steaks we had carried all that way. They were unbelievably delicious, but gone in a few bites. John hooked a grayling, which likewise disappeared in a hurry. To go with the steak we had a huge portion of rice with the last of the gravy, the last of the carrots, the last soup, and the last pudding—made with the last of the Klim.

John never did find time to bake that pie. After the feast he made a bannock out of the last of the flour and a jam out of the last of the raisins and the last of the sugar. The bannock and raisin jam would do for breakfast and lunch. If we were still traveling the day after that, our meals would be of odds and ends—but at least there would be *something* to eat.

Return

August 25

BOTH OF US slept poorly. We were too excited at the prospect of reaching Snowdrift. It was the reaction of a kid who was about to go on an excursion to an amusement park. Since we were both awake, we crawled out at four o'clock. We were on Browning Standard Time, strictly a local variety. My watch gained about two minutes a day, and although I had tried to remember to set it back by that amount each morning, the accumulated error over a period of eleven weeks was probably quite large. John's watch had gotten moisture in it and given up the ghost early in the trip.

In due time

It was stimulating to be up so early. Our luck with the weather seemed to be holding. There were rosy streaks in a partly cloudy sky, and no discernible wind. Warm sunrays slanted through the treetops.

Breakfast consisted of half the bannock and half the raisin jam, the last of the spanish rice, and tea. It was the largest breakfast we had had since we ran out of meat. Our mental outlook certainly was improved by having a respectable amount of food in our stomachs. We murmured and grunted our appreciation when our mouths were full, and between bites exclaimed over and over again how delicious it was. It tasted like an incredibly rich dessert, a treat of the highest order. We threw out superlatives with wild abandon, but nevertheless our vocabularies were not adequate for such an event.

Superlatives

We consulted the map once more, even though we both had practically memorized it. A lengthy discussion ensued about the chance of reaching Snowdrift, about how much food remained, and about how many meals we could make out of it should we not reach Snowdrift. We decided that we would travel until sundown if there was a reasonable chance of getting to Snowdrift by then; long hours would be preferable to spending another night out. We bolstered each other's spirits by remarking on what a snap the remaining two or three portages would be after what we had already been through. We seemed to alternate playing opposing roles. Usually it was John, the eternal optimist, who minimized the difficulties ahead and put out glowing predictions of how easily we would progress, while I demurred and served up cautionary remarks. But this time it was I who prophesied an easy jaunt to Snowdrift, while John worried about the remaining falls and rapids and, in particular, the possibility of becoming windbound on either Stark Lake or Great Slave itself.

Optimism, realism, doubt

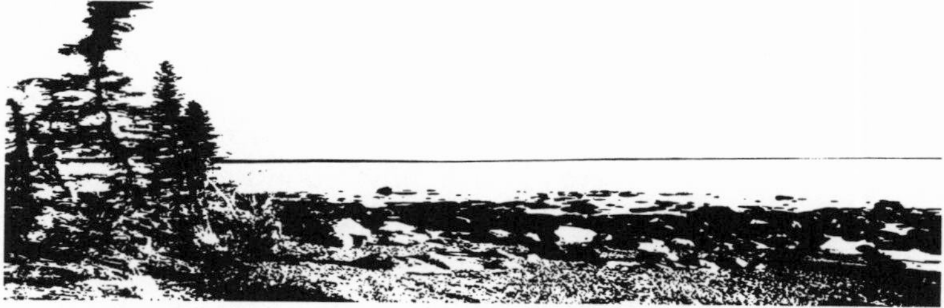

We packed our gear for what we hoped was the last time, and did the short portage to the base of the falls. The portage was mostly across bare rock, but nevertheless we thought we could detect a trail. Of course we very much wanted to detect a trail, for it would confirm that we were actually where we thought we were. At seven on the dot the canoe was loaded, and we pushed out into the river. If we and the map were correct, a two-mile paddle would bring us to the last falls. We went along slowly, swinging wide around the bends so as not to be abruptly caught up by swift current. But the falls did not materialize; it simply wasn't where it should have been. We checked the map once more, and took compass bearings up and down the river in an endeavor to locate our position exactly. We concluded that we had hit the river farther down than we thought. Evidently we came out somewhere between the last two falls, so that the falls we had just portaged around was the final one. It would be clear sailing the rest of the way. Suddenly I was wildly elated. I let out a whoop of joy, turned around to look at John, and announced: "We're home free!" He was grinning broadly and nodding his head.

Home free

"You could be right," he said. "You could be right." I really wanted to say something profound and deathless. But it was no use. The best thing I could do was to keep my mouth shut and wield the paddle. In times of great emotion, trite remarks will always come to the fore.

Another twenty minutes of paddling brought us to the mouth of the river. There was a mile-wide channel leading off to the east-northeast, with Stark Lake opening up beyond. We landed on a sandy point, got out the cameras, and took pictures of each other, the canoe, the water, sand, sky.

Author, mouth of the Snowdrift River, last morning of the trip. We landed on a sandy point and got out the cameras.

The moment of elation quickly passed; there was nothing to sustain it. Nor was I able to feel the satisfaction or even the relief I had thought would be forthcoming. I was conscious mainly of a weakness in my arms and legs, and my thoughts were of food. It was scarcely possible that we were almost to Snowdrift. We had been traveling so long that it had come to seem as though there would be no end to it. And now that the great moment was about to arrive, I was devoid of all passion. I was so weary of the nomadic life that I didn't even feel like putting out the effort required to cover the last few miles. I simply wanted it to be over and done with in an instant.

There was a noticeable east wind once we were out of the river. Long gentle rollers came up the channel toward us, and we thought it possible we would have trouble crossing the seven or eight miles of open water between the river's mouth and the narrow passage leading from Stark Lake to Great Slave. We shoved off again and paddled at a good speed, determined to plow on through no matter how the wind and water performed.

Before we had gone a mile we heard the sputtering of an outboard engine. An Indian man and a boy in a kicker-driven boat came up the channel toward us. They were the first people we had seen for seventy-four days. We passed at a distance of fifty yards. They stared at us with intense curiosity, and finally gave a perfunctory wave. We waved back in the same manner. The sight of them made me uneasy.

The threat of strangers

I felt an ill-defined trepidation, as though we were being threatened by some unknown force. When they were a tenth of a mile astern their engine died. I was startled, and frightened by the sudden silence.

John hissed at me in a stage whisper. "What are they doing?"

"I don't know," I replied without looking back. "Why don't you take a look?"

"*You* take a look," he said.

I looked over my shoulder, afraid of what I might see. The man and boy were bent over the engine, and were paying no heed to us.

"Engine trouble," I said, and felt safe again.

We paddled on. John remarked that since we hadn't spoken to them it was almost as if we never had met them. It was a matter of keeping our record intact; logically or not, we had neither expected nor desired to meet anyone before reaching the post at Snowdrift.

The wind and waves increased considerably when we got to the open lake. It was reminiscent of Tent Lake or some of the larger lakes early in the trip. We headed northwest, with the east wind blowing spray into the canoe and wetting my right side from the waist down. Paddling seemed to be a more drudging task than it ever was before. By ten we were ready to take an early break and have lunch. We pulled into a sheltered cove on a large island, and treated ourselves to the

The delight of an orgy

greatest feed we'd had since the best of the caribou orgies. We polished off the bannock and raisin jam, the last bacon bar, the remainder of the corn chowder, peas, and chicken meat cooked up together, and washed all of it down with many cups of tea. Remaining in our food bag were one serving apiece of cabbage and mashed potatoes, a small portion of rice, and four tea bags. In the event we didn't reach Snowdrift, we would be rather hungry by morning.

But to hell with tomorrow! Eat, drink, and be merry, gentlemen. What a delight it was to relax our discipline. The heat of the fire and the act of chewing and swallowing had me feeling drowsily voluptuous. Too bad I couldn't have dropped off to sleep in a warm bed, with a full belly, at that very moment. It would have been a fitting end to the trip.

Surfeited

The canoeing conditions worsened while we indulged in this sybaritic interlude. Despite our best efforts and the temporary protection offered by two small islands, we were driven due west, some fifty or sixty degrees off the desired course. When we reached the shore of the mainland we turned north and paddled parallel to it, keeping within twenty feet of land. We were running broadside to the waves, and the only way to make any progress was to stay in shallow water. I felt much put upon. An adverse wind was a cruel thing during the final hours of the trip.

We struggled around three small points, being continually splashed by waves and shipping a small amount of water. At three we left Stark Lake and got into the channel, where we were out of the wind. We easily negotiated two mild, shallow rapids—and we were in Great Slave Lake at last, with only a couple of miles to go. After covering half that distance we pulled into shore to spruce up a bit. We looked somewhat disreputable; and perhaps we were noticeable in other ways, too, by those so unfortunate as to be downwind from us. Without desiring it, we found ourselves caught up by the mores of our overdeveloped society—the mores we had so blithely peeled away over the past eleven weeks. One should be clean, one should be neatly dressed, one should put one's best foot forward.

Disreputable

John changed his shirt and pants, donning not clean ones but less dirty ones. My major concession was to splash some water on my face and run a comb through my hair. We dug deep into our gear and unearthed our billfolds and a letter from Walitski at Stony Rapids to the manager of the post at Snowdrift, setting forth the details of the rental agreement on the canoe. As soon as we were armed with cash, traveler's checks, and the appropriate document, we felt capable of handling any situation presented to us by the Outside.

Well armed

We pushed off for the last time, and at 4:15 came to the place called Snowdrift. There were two rows of Indians' houses, with the individual dwellings hooked together by a single wire for electricity, a church and school at the far end of the settlement, a long dock probing the ruffled water, a cluster of gasoline drums, and the buildings of the Hudson's Bay Company: the manager's house, the store, and two warehouses—trim and sturdy structures painted white with the traditional red roofs. The Red Ensign with its bold HBC stood out stiffly from atop the flagpole in the east wind. Beside the floatplane dock was a sign reading:

WELCOME TO SNOWDRIFT

Pop. 184
Dogs 191
Cats Nil

"CHAMBER OF COMMERCE"

Welcome, indeed. Snowdrift, we are here!

Amazing event

As we paddled along the shore and around the dock, the few Indians in sight dropped whatever they were doing and regarded us with amazement. Two white men, materializing out of the bush without warning, pushing a canoe through the water by muscle power alone. (What! No kicker?) An inexplicable phenomenon. By the time we ran the canoe up on the shore there were fifteen or twenty young men and boys standing on the dock, waiting for us.

We stepped onto the sand, shook hands vigorously, and offered each other heartfelt congratulations. We made a beeline for the store, surrounded by and trailing a group of boys. At the entrance to the store we engaged in a brief, ludicrous moment of excessive politeness: an Alphonse-and Gaston act of elbow-clutching, pushing, and pulling, as each tried to usher the other into the store. So as to share this historic moment we squeezed through the doorway together, bumping shoulders and the doorjambs as we went. We walked through the store to the office in the rear and introduced ourselves to the manager, Peter Jackson.

Making history

Due to some foul-up in communications he had not been expecting us. We were as much of a surprise to him as we were to the Indians. John and I both talked at once, explaining who we were, whence we had come, how long it had taken us, and trying to condense the entire scope and nature of the trip into a few phrases. But of course it couldn't be done. I had been talking to John, and John only, for so long that I wasn't able to communicate with anyone else. My sentences were poorly formed, the words came haltingly, and I repeated myself. A few minutes of this awkward, stumbling conversation sufficed for the amenities, and we returned to the store.

Cornucopia

The array of packaged and canned goods was at first overwhelming, but our attention was soon riveted on what was our most pressing desire—chocolate bars. We bought one each, discreetly nibbled at a square or two, and then, unable to control ourselves, gulped down the remainder; and bought another at once, and yet another. We gobbled five or six bars apiece in the next ten minutes. We traded the .303 cartridges we had found for eight dollars and some odd cents credit, and at once stocked up on food: crackers, cookies, preserves, peanut butter, a can of condensed milk, a two-pound bag of salt, three tins of sardines, a can of corned beef, a one-pound tin of butter, a pound of cheese, and ten or twelve more chocolate bars.

The store closed at 4:30. We sat on the steps of one of the warehouses, rapidly eating cookies and chocolate even as we cautioned each other to be abstemious. Peter's wife, Elma, had baked bread and biscuits. Peter invited us to dinner, and provided us with half a dozen biscuits and some marmalade to tide us over until the meal was ready. We bolted them in an instant, licked our lips, and found that our appetites had increased. At that moment we could have eaten a jackass stuffed with firecrackers.

Snowdrift. Indians' houses, the manager's house, the warehouse, and part of the store.

Gourmets at work

The dinner seemed like a banquet. At last, at last, at last we ate our fill—and then some. Two platefuls apiece, heaped to overflowing with meat, potatoes, two vegetables, as much bread, butter, and preserves as we could stuff into our gullets, and vast quantities of milk and coffee. We loaded ourselves to the point of physical discomfort; as a matter of fact, John couldn't finish his second plateful. But two hours later we had recovered sufficiently to put away two large slices of apple pie and two cups of hot chocolate apiece. So unable were we to resist temptation that we both eagerly accepted cigarettes when Peter offered them around. John was at last able to burn the taste of the food out of his mouth, and with my willpower gone I was on my way to becoming a smoker again.

Later in the evening Peter took us a couple of miles up the lake in his boat to the Frontier Lodge, a fishing camp. The owner of the camp, Jim St. Marie, had shut down for the season and was flying out the next day on a chartered plane to Yellowknife. He agreed to arrange for a plane large enough to accommodate the three of us and our baggage, and generously offered to split the cost right down the middle. The problem of how to get out of such a remote place being solved, we returned to the post, pitched our tent in the lee of a warehouse, and turned in for the night. We were bloated with too much food, but before dropping off to sleep we expressed the hope that Elma would feed us a large breakfast.

August 26

Anticlimax

THE TRIP HAD ENDED in a crashing anticlimax. We were emotionally empty. The delight and sense of achievement we had anticipated so long had not appeared. Nor was there any incentive other than food obsessions that could drag us from the tent in the morning. What it was that we had expected I could not remember. A brass band? Welcoming speeches? The keys to the city? Adulation of the raucous multitudes?— I did not know. We were left with the vague, rankling impression that we had been cheated of whatever it was we sought. We felt that there should have been, in some fashion or other, a grand and profound conclusion to our long journey, but there was nothing we could pinpoint. It had abruptly ended, expired, died, like the flame of a candle snuffed out between thumb and forefinger.

Nothing remained

Our canoe was high and dry. There was no gear to pack, no rapids to wade, no white-capped lake to cross, no agonizing portage awaiting us. We had lost the firm orientation we had while traveling in the wilderness, and had nothing with which to replace it. When we beached our canoe for the final time we lost our purpose in life. Nothing remained, and I did not know what we would do.

How could it be that there was neither contentment nor exhilaration? There was no answer. We felt only apathy and weariness. We were unable to decipher our own emotions, nor to have the least understanding of how it could have come to that. How strange it all was.

Elma prepared a huge breakfast: fruit juice, canned fruit, dry cereal, eggs, bacon, an entire loaf of bread, and marmalade and raspberry preserves. We polished it off with ease, then drank many cups of coffee while hoping wistfully that Elma would notice the empty table and trot out some more food.

We engaged in desultory picture-taking, and set up an open-air secondhand store where we attempted to sell the canvas fly, the tarps, the pots and pans, and the remaining axe to whatever Indians were interested and had the money.

Indian children at Snowdrift. They were very friendly and spoke fair English. Their parents were aloof and spoke little English, and the old people knew only key words: rifle, moose, canoe.

Gluttony

The Indians are always broke at the tail end of summer, and we were lucky to deal off everything except the cooking gear. But most of the time we nibbled the food we had bought the day before. When I wanted to go a hundred yards from the food to snap a picture, I took eight cookies with me—four to get me there and four to bring me back to where I could grab another handful. We berated each other for our unabashed gluttony, but our mouths were full as we spoke.

Idolatry

During the afternoon we browsed through two months of newspapers and some back copies of magazines. The news was all too familiar. The same stupidities were being committed in precisely the same way and with the same fervor and idolatry. At first glance it seemed that the world's troubles had become exaggerated, but that was undoubtedly because we had been away from them for so long.

Craziness

Instantaneous mass communication proves one thing only: very few people have anything important to say—and that, seldom. The papers could have been from a year or ten years earlier; were they not dated we would not have been the wiser. All the reports were of wars, murders, suffering, catastrophes—nothing new at all. The one real surprise was that the Republicans had nominated Goldwater. What folly! We were amazed and horrified. Perhaps the inhabitants of the Banana Belt had fallen prey to a major psychosis, and we would have been safer and far better off if we had gone back into the bush.

But that was neither possible nor practical; we had to return to take up our normal lives again. All that remained was the mechanical business of getting home. At five o'clock Peter and Elma ran us up to the Frontier Lodge again. A de Havilland "Beaver" arrived on schedule. We loaded our gear, thanked the Jacksons for their kind hospitality, said quick goodbyes, and were borne away across the glistening lake and the dark green forest.

John took a few pictures from the air, but we were jaded and had no eyes for the vast, lonely territory beneath us. On the hour-and-ten-minute flight I munched a couple of chocolate bars and John gnawed on a piece of smoked trout. When we arrived in Yellowknife we checked into a hotel, showered, put on the clean clothes we had carried with us the entire summer, and headed for the nearest restaurant. The legacy of our trip to the North was good appetite. We were ravenous.

Aftermath

August 27–September 9

THE ROMANTIC INTERMEZZO was over; the chimerical summer was behind us. Forty-eight hours after the trip ended we were scarcely able to believe that we had done it. Rather it seemed that we had thumbed through a picture book of a journey taken by two remote acquaintances.

Our lives had been torn up by the roots; there was no stability and no permanence. The leap back into the mechanical world was as abrupt and complete as was our departure from it eleven weeks earlier. Once again a host of gaudy, strident impressions obliterated all memory. The present dominated; the past was but shadows and echoes.

Yellowknife was like a small midwestern American town transplanted in the forests and glacial bedrock of the Northwest Territories. It required a conscious effort to realize that we were in Canada rather than the United States. Practically everything that caught our attention was of American origin or style. The most striking features of this outpost of the industrial, economic world were the automobiles. Despite the best efforts of designers to achieve a sleek, elegant effect, the cars seemed angular, squat, lumpish. They had a harsh, menacing look to them, and moved along the streets in a crabbed fashion. Without legs or any other visible means of locomotion, they appeared to be of other-worldly origin.

Sinister automobiles

We rode the bus to Edmonton, a 1,000-mile trip that took thirty-two hours. We picked up John's car, and steered westward. There followed a rapid tour through Jasper National Park, Banff and Lake Louise, Yoho, Glacier, and Mt. Revelstoke national parks, along the Fraser River, on to Vancouver, and then to Seattle. There was little joy in any of it. We did it because we had planned it, and did not even conceive of altering the arrangement. The food obsessions were still with us. We consumed three large meals a day, had many snacks between meals, and were unable to pass a bakery without stopping for a sackful of tarts, rolls, and cookies.

Do not pass bakeries!

We parted company in Seattle fifteen days after our arrival at Snowdrift. Both of us felt that much had been left unsaid, that we had failed to make a proper summation of the trip in terms that had meaning and value for either of us. And we despaired of ever imparting to anyone else more than a superficial, barren description of the wanderers' progress through the solitude and cold beauty of the North.

The solitude and cold beauty of the North.

Winter

LITTLE BY LITTLE, in the weeks and months that followed, the worth and significance of our travels rose to the surface of consciousness. We did it for ourselves alone, and it paid off handsomely. For the first and only time, all facets of our lives joined to form a coherent whole. Our minds and energies were directed exclusively toward the attainment of a clear and logical goal. Such an experience does not bear comparison with our normal lives, where all imaginable goals forever recede into a blurred and misty future—an existence where one seems to have merely a handful of loose, disconnected threads that can never be tied together.

The preoccupations, distractions, and confusions of the daily round are many, and often to serve to wash away the past. Yet I am able to sit at the ocean's edge, squinting in the bleak brightness of winter sunlight, and readily bring to mind a panorama of northern landscape. There are evenings of endless twilight; dark-blue lakes flecked with white; layers of pale green pollen swelling and falling on the water's surface; a perfect arc of tree-lined beach curving away to a point of black rock; the stark, exposed loneliness of the Barrens; the

aurora flickering and waving across the zenith above the Snowdrift River; white water leaping and churning down a rapids on its way to Hudson Bay or the Northern Ocean. For most of the year it is all at rest, glistening and frozen in a subarctic winter, but once again—and forever—the brief weeks of summer will erupt in a reckless rush of life.

Time and distance have blurred my memory, so that I recall even the hardship and exhausting labor with pleasure, with fondness. I remember it as rest and peace and quiet. This is the true legacy of the journey: a lasting sense of tranquillity and permanence that I have found in no other place and that can be had in no other way.

Like all others and all else, I have come full circle—from dream to reality and back. But perhaps it is not quite full circle, for nothing can ever be the same. Now the desire for freedom is strong again. I am not reconciled to this life, and soon I hope to roam once more in my private wilderness.

Appendix

General Equipment

tent and stakes
waterproof fly 9 x 10
ground cover
two tarps 7 x 9
two boxes
three Woods bags
camp grill
aluminum cooking set
ten-inch frying pan
two bread pans
stainless steelware
two spatulas
can opener
three rolls aluminum foil
roll of plastic wrap
two plastic soup bowls
Primus stove
aluminum fuel bottle
flashlight
hammer
three pounds assorted nails
two fishing tackle
shovel
.22 rifle
.270 rifle
15 bottles insect repellent
bug bomb
scouring powder
liquid detergent
pot scrubber

Personal Equipment (each)

sneakers
raincoat and hat
cap
sleeping bag
air mattress
axe
hunting knife
compass
pack frame
leather work gloves
wool gloves
parka
sweater
three pairs twill pants
three twill shirts
wool shirt
seven pairs cotton socks
seven pairs sweat socks
six sets underwear
set of thermal underwear
hiking boots
wading boots

Food List

ten pounds flour
ten packs yeast
baking powder
nine pounds sugar
eleven pounds oatmeal
ten tins jam (4 lbs each)
baking soda
three pounds salt
garlic salt
small can pepper
three boxes kitchen matches
one small can of Klim
ten pounds lard
fifty dehydrated soups
thirty puddings
two boxes raisins
three small boxes instant rice
120 servings instant potatoes
five packs brown gravy mix
five packs chicken gravy mix
120 tea bags
four concentrated lemon juice
three bags lemon drops
3,000 saccharine tablets
ten pounds cheese
six loaves bread
ten bacon bars
fifty Tropical chocolate bars

Freeze-dried meats
five cans diced ham
one can meat balls
one can pork chops
one can beef steaks

Number of servings of dehydrated foods from Dri Lite

30 spanish rice
30 vegetable stew
30 corn chowder
30 chili and beans
30 beans
10 macaroni and cheese
30 ground beef
20 ground chicken
24 applesauce
24 fruit cocktail
24 peach slices
24 pear slices
24 fruit mix
24 pitted prunes
8 date bits
8 fig slices
10 eggs
30 potato cubes
36 peas
30 green beans
30 corn
18 carrot slices
16 cabbage

A Northern Bibliography

The following list of works is not intended to be comprehensive. The major focus is on exploration, travel, and description in the mainland Northwest Territories from the earliest times to the present. I have also included several items concerning canoe travel in Labrador early in this century. Some of these books are scarce, and will likely not be found outside of libraries in major universities and large cities. I believe that the majority of them will be found as readily in the United States as in Canada. Fortunately a number of the classic works have been reprinted, and I have indicated those of which I am aware. For those who wish to expand their reading to include the vast literature of arctic exploration, the reference volume to consult is *The Exploration of Northern Canada, 500 to 1920, A Chronology*, by Alan Cooke and Clive Holland. You should note that a few of the items in this list are things that I have not seen. I am taking them on faith from people who are more knowledgeable than I about the literature of the Northwest Territories.

BACK, George. *Narrative of the Arctic Land Expedition to the Mouth of the Great Fish River, and Along the Shores of the Arctic Ocean, in the Years 1833, 1834, and 1835*. London: John Murray, 1836. Reprinted by M. G. Hurtig Ltd., Edmonton, 1970. The first descent—and ascent—of the Back River. Two winters at Fort Reliance at the northeastern end of Great Slave Lake.

BELL, James M. *Far Places*. Toronto: Macmillan, 1931. Good material on Great Slave Lake and Great Bear Lake.

BERTON, Pierre. *The Mysterious North*. New York: Alfred A. Knopf, 1956. Interesting popular accounts of the Yukon, the South Nahanni River, the Arctic, Yellowknife, Labrador, and more, as they were in the late forties and early fifties. Good historical background material, good photos, good index.

BETHUNE, W. C. *Canada's Western Northland. Its History, Resources, Population and Administration*. Department of Mines and Resources. Ottawa: King's Printer, 1937.

BIRKET-SMITH, Kaj. *The Eskimos*. London: Methuen, 1936. Reprinted by Crown Publishers, New York, 1971. Interesting accounts of the Caribou Eskimo by an expert on the subject.

BIRKET-SMITH, Kaj. *Geographical Notes on the Barren Grounds*. The Fifth Thule Expedition, 1921–1924, v. 1, no. 4. Copenhagen: Gyldendal, 1933.

BLANCHET, Guy. *Great Slave Lake Area and Northwest Territories*. Ottawa: F. A. Acland, printer to the King, 1926.

BLANCHET, Guy. *Keewatin and Northeastern Mackenzie*. Department of the Interior. Ottawa: F. A. Acland, printer to the King, 1930.

BLANCHET, Guy. *Search in the North*. Toronto: The Macmillan Company of Canada Limited; New York: St. Martin's Press, 1960. The first attempt, in 1928, to search for minerals in the Canadian North by air. Trial and error; crashes; rescues. Good story.

BURWASH, L. T. *Canada's Western Arctic*. Ottawa: F. A. Acland, printer to the King, 1931.

BUTLER, William Francis. *The Great Lone Land. A Narrative of Travel and Adventure in the North-West of America*. London: Sampson Low, Marston, Low, & Searle, 1872. Reprinted by M. G. Hurtig, Ltd., Edmonton, 1968. A romantic and colorful account of the Red River Expedition and other travels and adventures in western Canada. Butler got as far west as Rocky Mountain House on the North Saskatchewan River.

BUTLER, William Francis. *The Wild North Land. Being the story of a Winter Journey, with dogs, across northern North America*. This is a first-rate adventure story of a winter journey to British Columbia, Oregon, and the Pacific. Butler went from Fort Garry on the Red River of the North via Lake Athabasca, Peace River, and the Fraser River.

CALEF, George. *Caribou and the Barren Lands*. Toronto: Firefly Books Limited, 1981. Outstanding photography and text by a noted wildlife biologist.

CAMERON, Agnes Dean. *The New North; Being Some Account of a Woman's Journey Through Canada to the Arctic*. New York and London: D. Appleton and Company, 1910. Reprinted simultaneously by Western Producer Prairie Books, Saskatoon, and University of Nebraska Press, Lincoln and London, 1986. Not an exploring or wilderness journey, but interesting for its observations of life and travel in 1908. Cameron went from Edmonton to the Mackenzie via the usual route: the Athabasca, Slave, and Mackenzie rivers, varying the route on her return via Peace River and Lesser Slave Lake. Please note: Get the original edition if you can; the reprints lack most of the photos.

CAMSELL, Charles. *Son of the North*. Toronto: Ryerson Press, 1954. A very interesting autobiography of a man who was born in Fort Liard in 1876, the son of a Hudson's Bay Company officer. He was many things during his life: prospector, teacher, explorer, geologist—which activities included forty-four years in the Civil Service.

CHOQUE, Charles. *Joseph Buliard, Fisher of Men*. Churchill, Manitoba: R. C. Episcopal Corp., 1987. Buliard was a Back River priest.

CHRISTIAN, Edgar Vernon. *Unflinching, a Diary of Tragic Adventure*. London: J. Murray, 1937. Reprinted as *Death in the Barren Ground*, ed. by George Whalley. Ottawa: Oberon Press, 1980. Christian was a nephew of John Hornby, the by now legendary Englishman who spent more than twenty years wandering in the North. In the fall of 1926 Hornby took Christian, then eighteen years old, and Harold Adlard, age twenty-six, to winter with him on the Thelon River. Christian's diary *Unflinching* is the record of that winter and of the starvation and death of the three men. This should be read in conjunction with Malcolm Waldron's *Snowman*, and with the book that ties all of it together—George Whalley's *The Legend of John Hornby*.

CLARKE, C. H. D. *A Biological Investigation of the Thelon Game Sanctuary*. Ottawa: Canada Department of Mines and Resources, 1940. Bulletin no. 96, National Museum of Canada, 135 pages. A scarce item, with a good bibliography.

COPLAND, Dudley A. *Coplalook*. Winnipeg: Watson & Dwyer, 1985. Copland was the chief trader for the Hudson's Bay Company from 1923 to 1939.

CUNDY, Robert. *Beacon Sec*. London: Eyre & Spottiswoode, 1970. British kayaks on the Back River. Unusual trip by an inexperienced crew to Cape Britannia in search of Franklin relics.

D'AOUST, Gus. *Those Were the Days That I lived and Loved*. St. Pierre, Manitoba: Alix Harpelle, 1984. Gus was a Barrenlands trapper. Anecdotal accounts of real life by a man talking straightforwardly about what he did and what it was like, with no need to gild the lily.

DOUGLAS, George M. *Lands Forlorn, A Story of an Expedition to Hearne's Coppermine River*. New York and London: G. P. Putnam's Sons, 1914. A gem—not to be missed. To the Coppermine River and Coronation Gulf via Great Slave Lake, the Mackenzie River, Great Bear Lake, Dease River, and the Dismal Lakes, in 1911. John Hornby is here, too. Includes 180 photographs of remarkably good quality for the time.

DOWNES, P. G. *Sleeping Island*. Toronto: Longmans, Green & Company, 1943. New York: Coward-McCann, Inc., 1943. Reprinted by Western Producer Prairie Books, Saskatoon, 1988. Excellent narrative of one man's journeying in the Manitoba-NWT boundary area in the late 1930s.

FRANKLIN, John. *Narrative of a Journey to the Shores of the Polar Sea, in the Years 1819, 20, 21, and 22*. London: John Murray, 1823. Reprinted by M. G. Hurtig Ltd., Edmonton, 1970. A classic of determination, hardship, suffering, and death in the finest British nineteenth-century tradition.

FRANKLIN, John. *Narrative of a Second Expedition to the Shores of the Polar Sea in the Years 1825, 1826, and 1827*. London: John Murray, 1828. Reprinted by M. G. Hurtig Ltd., Edmonton, 1971.

FRENCH, Francis Henry. *Report of the Bathurst Inlet Patrol, Royal Northwest Mounted Police, 1917–1918*. Ottawa: King's Printer, 1919.

GILDER, William Henry. *Schwatka's Search; sledging in the Arctic in quest of the Franklin Records*. London: Sampson Low, Marston, Searle, and Rivington; New York: C. Scribner's Sons, 1881. Reprinted by Abercrombie & Fitch, New York, 1966. Sledging in the region north of Baker Lake.

HANBURY, David T. *Sport and Travel in the Northland of Canada*. New York: The Macmillan Company; London: Edward Arnold, 1904. Another classic. In 1899 Hanbury traveled from Hudson Bay to Great Slave Lake via Chesterfield Inlet, Baker Lake, the Thelon River, the Hanbury River (named for him), Clinton-Colden Lake, and Artillery Lake. He was the first white man to travel the upper Thelon and the Hanbury. In 1901–2, starting from Edmonton, Hanbury did the 1899 trip from west to east, then went from Baker Lake to the Arctic coast via Pelly Lake, along the coast to Kent Peninsula and the Coppermine River. Then to the Mackenzie River via Dismal Lakes, Dease River, Great Bear Lake, and Great Bear River.

HARRINGTON, Richard. *The Face of the Arctic*. New York: Henry Schuman, 1952. Graphic photos of starving Caribou Eskimo near Padlei.

HEARNE, Samuel. *A Journey from Prince of Wales's Fort in Hudson's Bay to the Northern Ocean . . . in the Years 1769, 1770, 1771, & 1772*. London: A. Strahan and T. Cadell, 1795. The most easily found reprint probably is the one edited by Richard Glover. Toronto: The Macmillan Company of Canada Limited, 1958. Hearne might be termed the Marco Polo of his times. In two and one half years he traveled nearly 5,000 miles—most of it on foot—as the sole white man with bands of Indians. Hearne was the first European to reach the Arctic coast in western Canada by land, thus proving once and for all that there was no Northwest Passage to be found westward from Hudson Bay.

HOARE, W. H. B. *Conserving Canada's Musk-Oxen. Being an account of an investigation of THELON GAME SANCTUARY, 1928–29*. Ottawa: F. A. Acland, King's Printer, 1930.

HODGINS, Bruce W. and Hobbs, Margaret, ed. *Nastawgan. The Canadian North by Canoe & Snowshoe*. Toronto: Betelgeuse Books, 1985. Fourteen essays. Good historical summaries by writers who know their material.

HOUSTON, C. Stuart, ed. *Arctic Ordeal. The journal of John Richardson, surgeon-naturalist with Franklin, 1820–1822*. Kingston and Montreal: McGill-Queen's University Press, 1984. The first publication of a journal written more than 160 years earlier. A thorough, professional work, illustrated with evocative pen-and-ink sketches. The editor's analysis, commentary, appendices, notes, and index are excellent.

HOUSTON, C. Stuart, ed. *To the Arctic by canoe, 1819–21: The Journal and Paintings of Robert Hood, Midshipman with Franklin*. Montreal: McGill Queen's University Press, 1974.

HUBBARD, Mina Benson. *A Woman's Way Through Unknown Labrador; an account of the exploration of the Nascaupee and George rivers*. London: John Murray, 1908. See also the two books by WALLACE.

HUNTER, Archie. *Northern Traders, caribou hair in the stew*. Victoria: Sono Nis Press, 1983. Hunter came to Canada in 1924, at age eighteen, as an apprentice clerk for the Hudson's Bay Company. For thirty-five years he managed various HBC posts in the arctic and sub-arctic, and in Manitoba, Saskatchewan, Ontario, and British Columbia—Repulse Bay, Wager Bay, Baker Lake, Churchill, Lac du Brochet, etc. Anecdotal, chatty.

INGSTAD, Helge. *The Land of Feast and Famine*. New York: Alfred A. Knopf, 1933. Trapping and travel east of Great Slave Lake.

KING, Richard. *Narrative of a Journey to the Shores of the Arctic Ocean, in 1833, 1834, and 1835; under the command of Capt. Back, R.N.* 2 vols. London: Richard Bentley, 1836. King was surgeon and naturalist to the expedition. He was a very observant man. There are excellent, detailed descriptions of the flora and fauna, Eskimos and their habits, clothing, victuals, etc., and of the scenery.

KITTO, F. H. *The North West Territories 1930*. Department of the Interior. Ottawa: F. A. Acland, King's Printer, 1930.

LAMB, W. Kaye, ed. *The Journals and Letters of Sir Alexander Mackenzie*. Cambridge: University Press, 1970.

LOPEZ, Barry. *Arctic Dreams. Imagination and Desire in a Northern Landscape*. New York: Charles Scribner's Sons, 1986. An outstanding recent book: informed, thoughtful, civilized. If you're unsure where your interests lie, or don't have the time for extensive reading about the North, then you can't do better than to read this book.

MACKENZIE, Alexander. *Voyages from Montreal, on the River St. Laurence, through the continent of North America, to the frozen and Pacific oceans; in the years 1789 and 1793*. London: T. Cadell, 1801. Reprinted a number of times, most recently by M. G. Hurtig Ltd., Edmonton. See LAMB, above.

MALAHER, Gerald. *The North I Love*. Winnipeg: Hyperion Press, 1984. Northern Manitoba stories from 1922 on.

MALLET, Thierry. *Glimpses of the Barren Lands*. New York: Revillon Frères, 1930. Short, interesting essays.

MALLET, Thierry. *Plain Tales of the North*. New York: Revillon Frères, 1925; New York and London: G. P. Putnam's Sons, 1926. Fifty succinct tales and episodes of animals, humans, and life in the North, by the then head of Revillon Frères.

MARSH, Donald B. *Echoes From a Frozen Land*. Edmonton: M. G. Hurtig Ltd., 1987. Marsh was a Christian missionary at Eskimo Point for eighteen years beginning in 1926.

MASON, Michael H. *The Arctic Forests*. London: Hodder & Stoughton Limited, 1924. Ethnology, history, natural history, and hunting.

MCCONNELL, Richard George. *Report on an exploration in the Yukon and Mackenzie Basins, N.W.T.* Geological and Natural History Survey of Canada. Part D. Annual Report, vol. 4, 1888–89. Montreal: William Foster Brown & Co., 1891. McConnell wintered at Fort Providence, and in the summer of 1888 went down the Mackenzie, across the Peel River Portage, down the Porcupine, up the Yukon, over Chilkoot Pass, down to Juneau, and back to Victoria. Some parts of this report are scientific, but there is much detailed travel information and observation.

MCKAY, John W. *Arctic Adventure, a Kazan River Journal*. Toronto: Betelgeuse Books, 1983. Daily journal of a party of eight, down the Kazan from Kasba Lake to Baker Lake in 1982.

MERRICK, Elliott. *True North*. New York: Charles Scribner's Sons, 1933. "One muggy night just before a thunderstorm, I sat up in my bed and hammered my fist on the wall and screamed in my mind, 'I'm getting out.' And I got out." Escape from New York to Labrador in the early 1930s.

MORSE, Eric W. *Freshwater Saga. Memoirs of a Lifetime of Wilderness Canoeing in Canada*. Toronto and London: University of Toronto Press, 1987. Morse was the pioneer of the recent (the past twenty-five years) recreational canoeing in the Barrens. There is much of interest here for the summer canoeist concerning routes, conditions, equipment.

MORSE, Eric W. *Fur Trade Canoe Routes of Canada/Then and Now*. Ottawa: National and Historic Parks Branch, 1969.

MOWAT, Farley. *People of the Deer*. Boston: Little, Brown and Company, 1952.

MOWAT, Farley. *The Desperate People*. Boston: Little Brown, 1959.

MOWAT, Farley, ed. *Tundra. Selections from the great accounts of Arctic land voyages*. With illustrations and maps. Toronto: McClelland and Stewart, 1973. The best anthology.

MUNSTERHJELM, Erik. *The Wind & the Caribou*. Toronto: Macmillan, 1953. An enjoyable, simply-written book by a trapper.

PATTERSON, R. M. *The Dangerous River*. New York: W. Sloane Associates, 1954; Sidney, B.C.: Gray's Publishing, 1972. Up the South Nahanni in the late 1920s in search of legendary lost gold. Staying to trap and live and discover riches of a different sort.

PELLY, David F. *Expedition: An Arctic Journey Through History on George Back's River*. Toronto: Betelgeuse Books, 1981. History, adventuring, and canoeing. Selections from Back's journals; Hudson's Bay Company history; and a 1977 trip down the Back.

PIKE, Warburton. *The Barren Ground of Northern Canada*. London: Macmillan and Co., 1892. New York: E. P. Dutton & Company, 1917. Reprinted by Arno Press, New York, 1967. Among other things, Pike in 1890 went down the Back River as far as Beechey Lake, only the second party after George Back to have traveled on the river.

PIKE, Warburton. *Through the Subarctic Forest. A record of a canoe journey from Fort Wrangel to the Pelly Lakes and down the Yukon River to the Behring Sea*. London and New York: Edward Arnold, 1896.

RAE, John. *Narrative of an Expedition to the Shores of the Arctic Sea in 1846 and 1847*. London: T. & W. Boone, 1850.

RAFFAN, James and Horwood, Bert, ed. *Canexus, the Canoe in Canadian Culture*. Toronto: Betelgeuse Books, 1988. Sixteen essays.

RAFFAN, James, ed. *Wild Waters. Canoeing Canada's Wilderness Rivers*. Toronto: Key Porter Books, 1986. Eight accounts of canoe travel on northern rivers. Beautifully illustrated.

RASMUSSEN, Knud. *Across Arctic America*. New York and London: Putnam's Sons, 1927. Rasmussen was *the* expert on Eskimo ethnology. He was part Eskimo himself and traveled extensively with them, recording many eloquent statements.

RUSSELL, Frank. *Explorations in the Far North. Being the report of an expedition under the auspices of the University of Iowa during the years 1892, '93 and '94*. Iowa City: The University, 1898. Slave River; Great Slave Lake; wintering at Fort Rae; musk-ox hunt to the vicinity of Contwoyto Lake; down the Mackenzie to the Beaufort Sea and along the coast to Herschel Island; from there on a whaler to San Francisco. Much ethnological material on Indians and Eskimos, and extensive notes on natural history.

SCOTT, Peter Markham. *Wild Geese and Eskimos; a journal of the Perry River Expedition of 1949*. London: Country Life; New York: Scribner's, 1951.

SETON, Ernest Thompson. *The Arctic Prairies. A canoe-journey in search of the caribou; being the account of a voyage to the region to the north of Aylmer Lake*. New York: Charles Scribner's Sons, 1911; London: Constable, 1912.

SIMPSON, Thomas. *Narrative of the Discoveries on the North Coast of America; effected by the officers of the Hudson's Bay Company during the years 1836–39*. London: Richard Bentley, 1843.

STEELE, Harwood. *Policing the Arctic. The story of the conquest of the Arctic by the Royal Canadian (formerly North-West) Mounted Police*. Toronto: Ryerson, 1936.

THOMPSON, David. *David Thompson's Narrative 1784–1812*. Ed. by Richard Glover. Toronto: Champlain Society, 1962. Thompson was one of the great cartographers of his day. He traveled widely and was a sympathetic observer of his surroundings.

TYRRELL, James Williams. *Across the Sub-Arctics of Canada. A journey of 3,200 miles by canoe and snowshoe through the Barren Lands*. London: T. Fisher Unwin; New York: Dodd, Mead and Company, 1898. Facsimile edition published by Coles Publishing Company, Toronto, 1973. First journey down the Dubawnt River, in 1893, through territory that was at that time still *terra incognita*.

WALDRON, Malcolm Thomas. *Snow Man; John Hornby in the Barren Lands*. Boston, New York: Houghton Mifflin Co., 1931. Should be read in conjunction with *Unflinching* by Edgar Christian, and *The Legend of John Hornby* by George Whalley.

WALLACE, Dillon. *The Long Labrador Trail*. Toronto: Fleming H. Revell Co.; New York: The Outing Publishing Company, 1907. The following volume should be read first.

WALLACE, Dillon. *The Lure of the Labrador Wild. The story of the exploring expedition conducted by Leonidas Hubbard, Jr.*. London: Hodder & Stoughton; New York, Chicago, Toronto: Fleming H. Revell Company, 1905.

WATT, Frederick B. *Great Bear, a Journey Remembered*. Yellowknife: Outcrop Ltd., 1980. The rush of 1932.

WHALLEY, George. *The Legend of John Hornby*. London: John Murray; Toronto: Macmillan, 1962.

WHITNEY, Caspar. *On Snow-shoes to the Barren Grounds. Twenty-eight hundred miles after musk-oxen and wood-bison*. London: Osgood, McIlvaine & Co., 1896.

WILSON, Clifford, ed. *North of 55°*. Toronto: Ryerson Press, 1954. A collection of fifteen essays and stories.

WILSON, Clifford, ed. *Northern Treasury, selections from The Beaver*. Toronto: Thomas Nelson, 1954.

You can order additional copies of this book directly from the publisher.
Price: — $14.95

Great West Books
P.O. Box 1028
Lafayette, CA 94549
(415) 283-3184

Also available from Great West Books:
Tahoe Place Names, the origin and history of names in the Lake Tahoe Basin, by Barbara Lekisch. Includes old names and Indian names, and a translation of a portion of the diary of Charles Preuss, cartographer with John C. Frémont. Paperback, 192 pages, 39 historic photos, extensive bibliography, 6 x 9.
Price: — $11.95

John Muir, In His Own Words, compiled and edited by Peter Browning. The essence of John Muir—332 quotations, with extensive index. Paperback, 112 pages, 6 x 9.
Price: — $9.95

Yosemite Place Names, the historic background of geographic names in Yosemite National Park, by Peter Browning. The book includes old names, Indian names, and accounts of the first tourist travel to Yosemite Valley, in 1855 and 1856. Paperback, 256 pages, 27 historic photos, extensive bibliography, 6 x 9.
Price: — $12.95

For durability and long life, these books have sewn bindings and are printed on acid-free paper.

Place Names of the Sierra Nevada, by Peter Browning, covering the area from Walker Pass to the northern boundary of Alpine County. 264 pages, 15 photographs, extensive bibliography, 6 x 9, sewn bindings. (Published by Wilderness Press, Berkeley, 1986.)
Price: — $12.95 for paperback; $19.95 for hard cover.

Shipping: — $1.50 for one book; add 50¢ for each additional book.
California residents please add the appropriate sales tax.
Check or money order, payable in U.S. funds, must accompany your order.

Text typeface: Palatino 10/13
Text paper: 60# Glatfelter B-16
Printing and binding: Thomson - Shore, Inc., Dexter, Michigan